LAST MINUTE

BRUNCH PARTY

Amelia Wasiliev

Photography Lisa Linder

LAST MINUTE

BRUNCH PARTY

Over 100 Inspiring Dishes to Feed Family
and Friends at a Moment's Notice

Hardie Grant

NORTH AMERICA

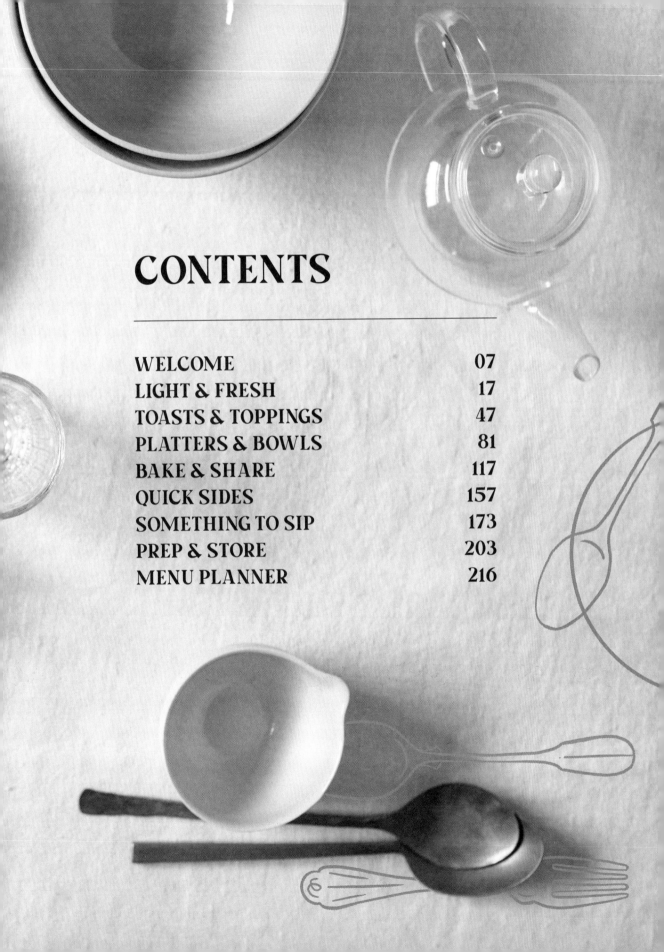

CONTENTS

WELCOME

I love so many breakfast foods, sometimes I think I could survive only on breakfast dishes, such as yogurt and fruit, granola, eggs, cured meats, toasts—breakfast on repeat all day. As someone who wakes up and doesn't like to eat immediately, brunch is my perfect mealtime. A combination of the best of breakfast and lunch, brunch encompasses sweet and savory and can be enjoyed at any time of the day. Sharing foods over morning tea and coffee with friends is one of my favorite styles of entertaining. Unlike a formal dinner party, brunch has a casual nature. In my mind it creates a relaxed and social atmosphere, allowing guests and hosts to unwind, indulge, and spend wholesome time connecting while enjoying a leisurely meal.

Last Minute Brunch Party helps to take the stress out of entertaining. Don't panic if guests arrive unannounced, this book will have you prepared to be a carefree, fabulous host in minutes. Set yourself up by stocking the pantry and having a few of these recipes already made in the freezer. From now on you'll always be ready for simple, fuss-free entertaining.

From the showstopping Crepe Layer Cake (page 112) to picnic-ready Sweet Potato Frittata Muffins (page 136), and brunch grazing boards (pages 94 to 98), your next brunch party is never far away. Throughout the book, you will also find simple tips and tricks to style your food, learn which recipes can be made ahead, and be given substitution options if you haven't got an ingredient on hand and don't have time to rush to the store.

The more you make these recipes, the easier they'll become, and before long you'll be adapting them and adding your own touches too. *Last Minute Brunch Party* helps you to utilize your everyday pantry, refrigerator, and freezer staples to create delicious, quick recipes that your guests will love.

KEY TO SYMBOLS

 VEGAN   DAIRY FREE   NF NUT FREE

 VEGETARIAN    GLUTEN FREE

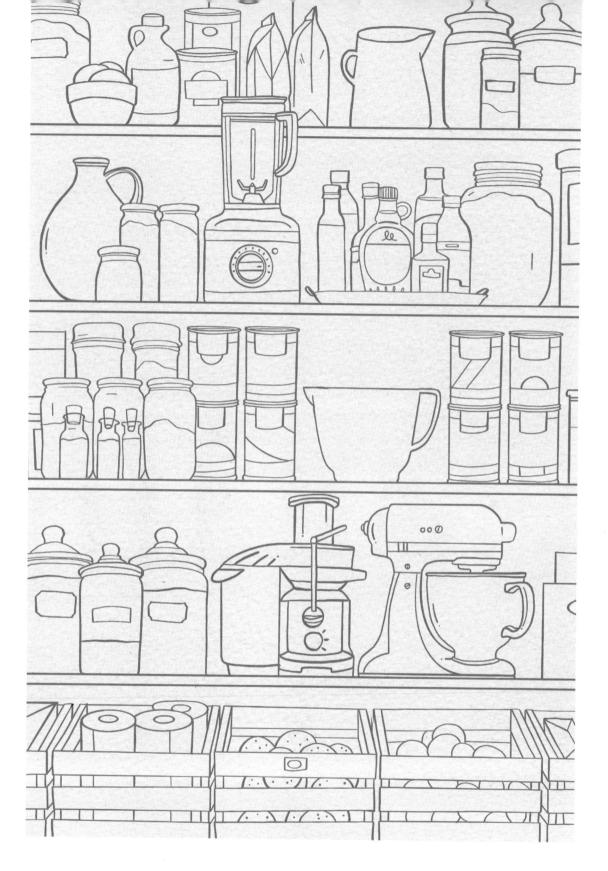

PANTRY STAPLES AND EQUIPMENT

The main ingredients used throughout this book are everyday ingredients that would probably be found in most home pantries. Likewise, most of the equipment used in this book should already be in your kitchen, but if not, you can easily adapt with different size pans or baking sheets. A few recipes require more specific items, but if you don't already own them there are ways you can get around it.

Baking essentials
Store baking ingredients, such as flour, sugar, baking powder, baking soda, and cocoa for up to 12 months in an airtight container. I always keep all-purpose white flour on hand, as it can be used in all recipes, and superfine and soft brown sugar for baking.

Nuts, seeds, grains
There is a huge selection of these available, and it's great to try different varieties. My top essentials are rolled oats, pumpkin seeds, slivered almonds, hazelnuts or pecans, chia seeds, and sesame seeds. Store nuts and seeds in airtight containers for up to 12 months.

Spreads, sauces, condiments
My top picks are peanut butter, honey, maple syrup, chocolate spread, as well as tomato sauce, mustards, including Dijon and wholegrain, hot sauce, and smoky bbq sauce.

Spices, flavorings
I use vanilla extract and vanilla beans constantly, but I also stock ground and whole cinnamon, dukkah, ground coriander, paprika, cumin, turmeric, and dried thyme.

Juicer
Fresh ingredients juiced make a delicious drink to pair with any meal but especially with tea, coffee, and brunch. If you don't have a juicer you can usually make these recipes in a blender or food processor. Blend the ingredients until as fine as they go, then use cheesecloth or a linen dish towel to hold the blended ingredients. Wrap the fabric around the blended mixture and squeeze all the juice into a bowl or pitcher.

Electric beater, stand mixer
While this equipment makes whisking and beating ingredients a lot less time-consuming, you can certainly still use the old-fashioned "by hand" method for all recipes in this book.

Sterilizing jars
For recipes such as pickled vegetables, compotes, curd, chutney, pesto, whipped feta, etc. that can be saved and stored to use later, it is best to use a sterilized jar. To sterilize jars, either wash them through a hot program in the dishwasher or wash them in soapy water, rinse in hot water, and place on a baking sheet, upright with the lid separate, and bake in a preheated oven at 250°F (130°C) for 20 minutes.

CHILLED ESSENTIALS

These are the staples that I keep in my refrigerator. I like to buy fresh seasonal vegetables, so I alter what I'm buying through the year, but I always have potatoes, sweet potatoes, garlic, and ginger too. Aside from fresh fruit and vegetables, these are my go-to basics to have on hand to make the most of the brunch recipes in this book, from Parmesan and smoked salmon to eggs and salami.

Eggs
Eggs will last a few weeks and are an ingredient I am never without. You can make so many things with eggs; a simple meal on their own or a delicious addition to many recipes.

Dairy such as milk, yogurt, cheese, butter, cream
Nowadays there are so many milk options. You'll probably have your own favorite on hand anyway, but it can be nice to try a few alternatives too. If you buy full-cream milk, perhaps try a coconut Greek-style yogurt. Butter is always in my refrigerator, and often heavy cream.

Cheeses
I like to have a couple of types of cheese in the refrigerator at all times. Bags of grated cheese are excellent for quick additions to recipes. Parmesan is a regular, and usually a type of Brie and a soft cheese, such as feta or goat cheese and cream cheese spread.

Bacon, cured meats, seafood
Many cured meats will last for up to a month in the refrigerator. Having a few packages on hand means that you are ready to whip up a delicious meal in no time at all. Bacon, salami, prosciutto, and smoked salmon are a few of my regulars.

Fresh herbs
I like to buy at least two types of fresh herbs every week or two. I rinse them, then wrap them in paper towels and place in an airtight container. They last well if stored this way.

Fresh vegetables
A few staples for brunch that I like to have on hand in the refrigerator are avocados, tomatoes, bell peppers, and seasonal greens.

Salad leaves
Baby spinach, arugula, and kale are my favorites. If stored in an airtight container in the refrigerator they will usually last for 2 to 3 weeks. They are an excellent addition to so many dishes.

Fresh fruit
As with vegetables, buy fruit that is in season. Try a few exotic fruits, such as figs, lychees, kiwis, melons, as they add a little extra to your parties. As I'm a big fruit eater, I like to have apples, bananas, and lots of citrus on hand too.

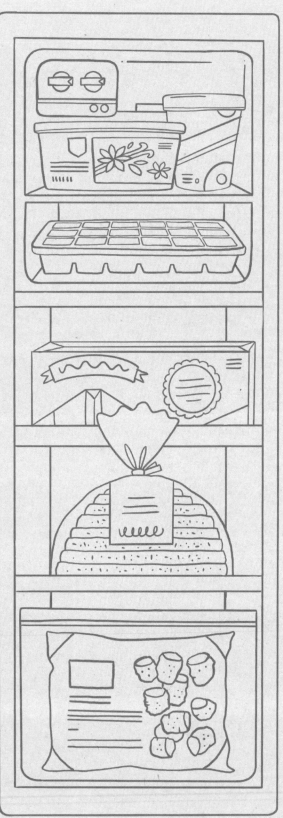

FREEZER ESSENTIALS

The freezer can be a great friend when planning ahead and also when there is no warning for mealtime entertaining. You can store ingredients for longer, and prep some recipes ahead such as the cookie dough on page 210 or the sheet pan pancakes on page 119.

Pastry

I like to have a package of puff pastry and phyllo pastry in the freezer at all times. They defrost easily and you can use them to make so many quick recipes, such as the Spinach Pie on page 131 or the Cinnamon Twists on page 148.

Cookie dough

Whether it's ready-to-bake cookie balls or a cookie dough log that you can slice, having dough in the freezer means warm cookies in less than 15 minutes. That is a definite win.

Frozen berries, fruit

You can make smoothies, frappes, ice creams, and many baked goodies very easily without a special trip to the store.

Breads, bagels

Bread doesn't last too long fresh so I always have a loaf of sliced sourdough and a selection of bagels in the freezer. You can defrost and eat them fresh or toast them immediately.

Herbs

Frozen herbs, such as cilantro, parsley, and mint, are always great to have in the freezer. You can buy herbs that are already frozen or you can freeze fresh herbs for later use. Chiles are also a great freezer option.

Frozen vegetables

I always like to keep a few frozen vegetables, such as frozen corn, spinach, and tater tots, in the freezer in case I have impromptu guests or if I don't have time to go to the store.

Ice cream

I try to have a tub of vanilla ice cream in the freezer as it's useful for quick desserts or to top drinks, such as the Bailey's Cream Affogatto on page 199.

Ice cubes

Ice cubes are an essential in the freezer as they are used in lots of the drinks in chapter six. You can store them in special ice-cube bags or trays.

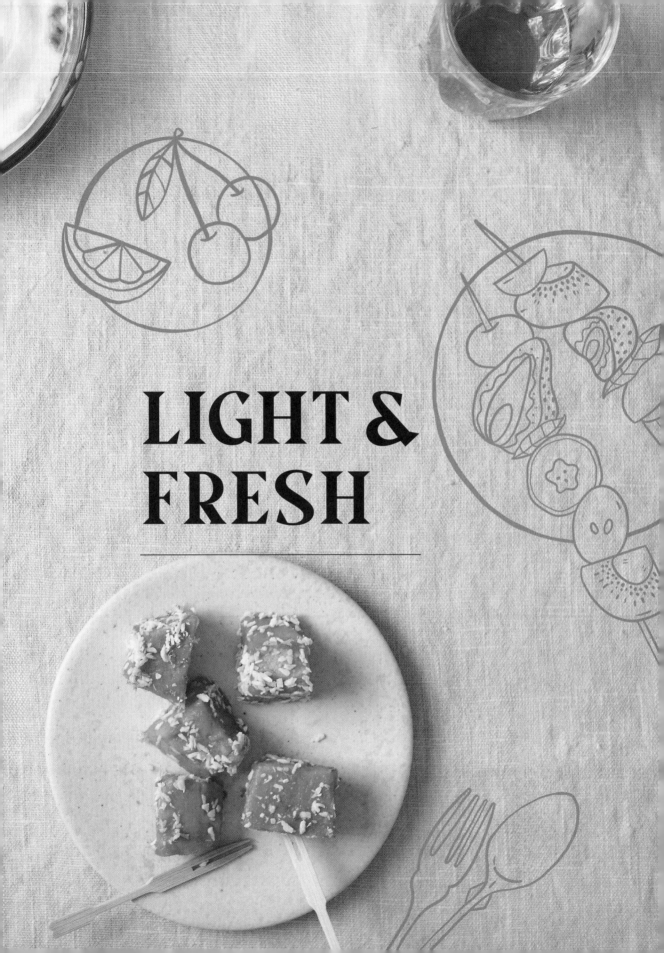

LIGHT & FRESH

POACHED VANILLA QUINCE YOGURT POTS

MAKES : 8 JARS
PREP TIME : 10 MINS
COOK TIME : 40 MINS

4 cups (900g) plain (or vanilla) thick yogurt
½ cup (40g) chopped pistachios

VANILLA QUINCE :

½ cup (120g) superfine sugar
1 vanilla bean, split in half lengthwise
Juice of ½ lemon
2 medium quince

The poached quince is enough for a 16-ounce (450g) jar, which is more than you need for this recipe, so store the rest in the refrigerator for up to 3 weeks. If you have all the components assembled, you can quickly make these cute yogurt pots and have them ready for your party.

For the quince, heat 2 cups (500ml) water, the sugar, vanilla, and lemon juice in a small saucepan and stir to dissolve the sugar. Cover and bring to a boil. Meanwhile, peel and core the quince and chop it into thin wedges. As you slice, add the quince to the poaching liquid. Once boiling, reduce the heat and simmer, covered, for 30 minutes, or until soft. Once cooked, let the quince and liquid cool completely before storing together in a 16-ounce (450g) jar in the refrigerator.

Fill 8 individual jars half full with thick yogurt. Add 2 slices of quince, then finish with a sprinkle of pistachios.

BAKED RHUBARB YOGURT POTS

MAKES : 8 JARS
PREP TIME : 10 MINS
COOK TIME : 20 MINS

4 cups (900g) plain (or vanilla) thick yogurt
½ cup (40g) chopped pistachios

RHUBARB :

½ pound (about 2 cups) rhubarb, leaves trimmed
½ cup (120g) superfine sugar
Finely grated zest and juice of 1 orange or lemon
¼ cup (60ml) pomegranate juice

If you can't find pomegranate juice, then just use another orange or lemon, but the pomegranate juice adds a great color.

Preheat the oven to 350°F (180°C).

Cut the rhubarb into 1-inch (2.5cm) pieces and place in a small baking dish. Add the sugar and mix to coat the rhubarb. Add the zest and juices, cover with foil, and roast for 15 minutes. Uncover, stir, and roast for another 5 minutes to reduce the syrup. Remove the rhubarb from the oven and stir, pressing some of the rhubarb pieces with the back of the spoon to mash and soak up the liquid. Let cool, then transfer to a 16-ounce (450g) jar and store in the refrigerator for up to 2 weeks.

Fill 8 individual jars half full with thick yogurt. Add a spoonful of the rhubarb, then finish with a sprinkle of pistachios.

MANGO YOGURT RIPPLE

For some reason fresh tropical fruits always make me think of vacations and relaxing by the pool or on the beach. This quick and easy dish will bring that to your party.

SERVES : 4
PREP TIME : 10 MINS
COOK TIME : 0 MINS

3 large mangoes
4 cups (900g) plain Greek yogurt
6-ounce (170g) can passion
    fruit pulp

Peel and slice the mango into long strips. Use a variety of shapes to get as much of the mango around the seed. Place one-third of the mango flesh in a blender and blend until smooth. In a large serving bowl, fold the yogurt together with the pureed mango, half of the passion fruit, and half of the remaining mango slices. Top with the last of the mango and passion fruit pulp.

SUBS :
When passion fruit are in season replace the canned passion fruit pulp with 4 large fresh passion fruit.

SALTY CITRUS SALAD

This is not your ordinary fruit salad but an excellent brunch accompaniment, or standalone dish. Use whatever citrus you have to make an equally eye-catching and flavorful dish.

SERVES : 4
PREP TIME : 15 MINS
COOK TIME : 0 MINS

3 oranges
2 blood oranges
1 ruby red grapefruit
2 clementines
4½ ounces (120g) ricotta salata
   or halloumi cheese
¼ cup (40g) roasted hazelnuts,
   chopped
Microgreens, for garnish (optional)

FOR THE DRESSING :
2 tablespoons olive oil
1 tablespoon citrus juice
   (leftovers from cutting the fruit)
2 teaspoons apple cider vinegar
½ tablespoon Dijon mustard
½ tablespoon honey
Pinch of sea salt flakes and
   black pepper

Cut the ends off all of the citrus, then, using a serrated or paring knife, slice the skin off the body of the fruit. Slice the flesh into circles so the core is in the center and each slice forms a flower shape. Cut any bigger slices into halves or quarters and layer the different slices of citrus onto a large flat plate. Save the juices as you cut and squeeze any fleshy pieces of skin scraps.

Add all the dressing ingredients to a small bowl and whisk to combine. Season with the sea salt and pepper to taste. Use a microplane to grate the cheese generously over the fruit, top with the chopped nuts, and pour over the dressing. Garnish with microgreens, if using.

SIMPLE SELF-SERVE
FRUIT PLATES

Fruit platters are a regular staple for any occasion. Here are some very easy but delicious ways to elevate your fruit serves. Start a brunch with one of these simple plates and some drinks and allow guests to help themselves.

MELON & PROSCIUTTO

SERVES : 8
PREP TIME : 5 MINS
COOK TIME : 0 MINS

1 whole cantaloupe melon
16 slices prosciutto
Basil leaves, for serving

Cut the cantaloupe melon in half and scoop out the seeds. Carefully remove the melon skin and cut each half into thick wedges. Each half should cut into about 8 wedges.

Wrap each melon wedge with a slice of prosciutto and arrange on a serving plate. You can do a few and leave the rest for your guests to wrap their own. Scatter with basil leaves. Cover and keep refrigerated until ready to serve.

PAPAYA WITH COCONUT

SERVES : 8
PREP TIME : 5 MINS
COOK TIME : 0 MINS

1 cup (250ml) thick yogurt of choice
2 tablespoons honey
1 papaya, seeded and peeled
Juice and finely grated zest of 1 lime
½ cup (30g) tightly packed flaked
    coconut, coarsely chopped

In a small bowl, mix the yogurt and honey together, then set aside. Cut the papaya into large cubes and place in a large shallow serving bowl. Pour the lime juice over and sprinkle with the coconut. Toss to combine, then top with the lime zest. Serve with toothpicks or little forks so guests can dip a square of papaya into the honey yogurt.

TIP :
When using citrus zest in dishes, make sure you use unwaxed fruit and wash and dry the skin before grating.

FRUIT SKEWERS

SERVES : 16
PREP TIME : 5 MINS
COOK TIME : 0 MINS

2 kiwi fruit

2 bananas, sliced into 8 pieces each

8 large strawberries, topped and
   halved, plus extra for serving

8 grapes, halved

16 mint leaves or small sprigs

16 medium wooden skewers

I like to eat the kiwi fruit skin but it does come down to personal preference. To prepare, cut the ends off the kiwi, then cut in half. Cut the halves into quarters to give you 8 pieces per kiwi. If you prefer you can remove the skin first.

Thread one of each type of fruit with a mint leaf onto each wooden skewer. Arrange the skewers on a large serving plate, cover, and keep cold in the refrigerator until ready to serve. Serve the skewers with a few extra strawberries.

SUB :

If grapes aren't in season, I often swap them for canned lychees instead, as I usually keep a can in the pantry.

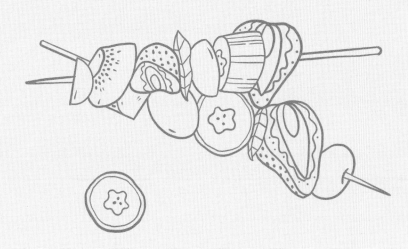

ACAI SMOOTHIE BOWL

SERVES : 4
PREP TIME : 10 MINS
COOK TIME : 5 MINS

4 tablespoons coconut flakes
½ pound (220g) frozen acai puree
    or 3 tablespoons acai powder
2 frozen bananas
2 cups (400g) coarsely chopped
    fresh pineapple
12 large strawberries, plus extra
    4 strawberries, sliced, for garnish
2 tablespoons vanilla protein
    powder (optional)
¾ cup (180ml) coconut yogurt
½ cup (60g) Granola (page 205)
2 tablespoons chia seeds

Smoothie bowls can look restaurant quality at home in no time at all. A trick I use is to prepare all the ingredients ready to blend before your guests arrive, keep in a container in the refrigerator, and then blend when ready to serve.

Preheat the oven to 350°F (180°C). Spread the coconut flakes out on a baking sheet and bake for 4 to 5 minutes, or until toasted.

Meanwhile, add the acai, bananas, pineapple, strawberries, protein powder, if using, and yogurt to a blender and blend until smooth, adding a little water as you blend if needed. Spoon the mix out into a bowl and top with the granola, sliced strawberries, toasted coconut, and chia seeds. Get creative and use the toppings to make a design or just group them together and place the strawberry on top.

CLEAN GREEN SMOOTHIE BOWL

SERVES : 4
PREP TIME : 10 MINS
COOK TIME : 0 MINS

1 ripe avocado, peeled and pitted
2 cups (300g) frozen mango
2 cups (60g) baby spinach leaves
2 tablespoons peanut butter
2 tablespoons honey
1 to 1½ cups (250 to 350ml)
    coconut water

FOR THE TOPPING :

1 mango
2 kiwi fruits
2 passion fruit
½ cup (50g) Cacao Nut Crunch
    (page 206)
2 tablespoons peanut butter

Try to make the mixture as thick as you can so it doesn't melt too quickly. Presentation is key, so take time neatly slicing the fruit and always make sure to have a crunchy addition to add some texture. Serve in one large bowl for guests to share, or if you have a little more time, individually top each bowl.

First, prepare your toppings by peeling the skin from the mango and kiwi fruit and thinly slicing the flesh. Scrape the passion fruit pulp into a small bowl and set aside.

For the smoothie, combine the avocado flesh, frozen mango, spinach, nut butter, honey, and 1 cup (250ml) of the coconut water in a blender and whizz to a thick smoothie consistency. You may have to scrape down the sides of the blender with a spoon a few times. Check the consistency as you go and gradually add more coconut water if needed. You want a thick consistency that holds its shape and is spoonable. Once the mixture is smooth, immediately divide between 4 bowls and arrange the prepared fruit on top. Sprinkle 2 tablespoons of the nut crunch over each bowl, drizzle with passion fruit pulp, and finish with a dollop of nut butter.

HERBY FIG SALAD

This simple salad is very quick to prepare. The addition of fruit gives a sweet, luxurious feel. I often swap both the herbs and the fruit for what I have on hand, and it's just as good with or without the cheese if you have any guests with special dietary requirements.

SERVES : 6
PREP TIME : 10 MINS
COOK TIME : 0 MINS

4½ ounces (120g) arugula
2 generous handfuls of mixed fresh
   herb leaves (basil, mint, flat-leaf
   parsley, dill)
1 small red onion
2 ounces (60g) Parmigiano
   Reggiano cheese
6 figs, at room temperature
Generous sprinkle of flaky sea salt

FOR THE DRESSING :
1 tablespoon olive oil
2 teaspoons red wine vinegar

Arrange the arugula and herbs on a large serving platter or shallow bowl. Peel and halve the onion and slice into thin wedges. Separate and sprinkle over the herb mix. Use a vegetable peeler to shave the cheese into large, thin pieces and toss over the salad leaves. Tear the figs into halves and then quarters, then arrange evenly over the salad before giving a good sprinkle of sea salt. Drizzle with olive oil and the vinegar and gently toss to mix.

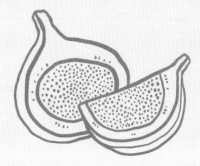

SUBS :
- 1 cup (150g) blackberries
- Swap the cheese for soft goat cheese
- ½ bulb fennel, shaved
- 2 nectarines, pitted and sliced into thin wedges

OVERNIGHT OATS WITH SLIVERED ALMONDS

In a last minute situation something that can be prepared the night before is always a winner. You can add different nuts and dried fruit to the overnight mix or keep it as simple as just the oats. The soaked oats take on a soft, creamy texture and the toppings add crunch. This also looks great served in a large bowl for guests to help themselves.

SERVES : 4
PREP TIME : 10 MINS
CHILL TIME : 2 HOURS
TO OVERNIGHT

1 cup (250ml) apple juice
2 cups (200g) rolled or porridge oats
1 teaspoon ground cinnamon
¼ cup (15g) flaked coconut
Juice of 1 orange
1 cup (250ml) thick Greek yogurt
2 green apples, grated (if grating ahead of time, coat the apples in lemon juice so they don't brown)
¾ cup (125g) mixed fresh berries
⅓ cup (35g) slivered almonds, toasted

Combine the apple juice, oats, cinnamon, and coconut in a large container and stir to combine. Cover and refrigerate for at least 2 hours or overnight to allow the oats to absorb the liquid.

On the day of serving, add the orange juice and a third of the yogurt to the soaked oats mixture and stir well to combine. Transfer the mix to a serving bowl and layer the remaining yogurt, grated apples, berries, and toasted nuts on top.

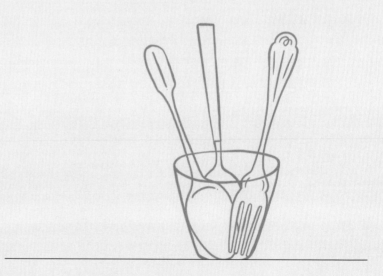

TIP :
Change the fruits and toppings according to the season or the ingredients you have on hand.

MAKE YOUR OWN MUESLI

While it's lovely to have a buttery, crunchy, toasted granola prepared ahead, sometimes it's just as tasty to eat a muesli that's made from raw ingredients, untoasted and simple. Making a muesli station is as easy as picking a few basics out of the pantry and refrigerator. I like to keep some of the ingredients in their storage jars and just add serving spoons. Make the options as simple or as complex as you like. Guests can help themselves and make a delicious bowl of muesli.

SERVES : 6
PREP TIME : 10 MINS
COOK TIME : 0 MINS

Fresh or stewed fruits, such
  as soaked prunes (see right)
  or Baked Rhubarb (page 19)
Rolled oats
Toasted slivered almonds, pecans,
  or macadamias, or coarsely
  chopped Brazil nuts
Dried fruits, such as apricots, flaked
  coconut, cranberries, currants,
  golden raisins
1 to 2 seeds / grains of choice,
  such as chia seeds, pumpkin
  seeds, sunflower seeds,
  bran flakes, rice bran cereal
Bowl of yogurt
Pitcher of milk, including a plant-
  based option

Before you set up your muesli station, if you are using soaked prunes, then place ¾ cup (100g) dried prunes in a small heatproof bowl or container, and pour boiling water over them so they are just covered. Let cool, then cover and store in the refrigerator until you are ready to serve. The water becomes a delicious prune juice / syrup and can be used in overnight oats or on yogurt.

TO ASSEMBLE :
Set the table with a stack of bowls, spoons, and napkins. Set up a pitcher of hot tea or coffee and instruct your guests to mix and match the ingredients to create their own muesli bowl. If you have time, you can even make little paper labels for the items or a menu.

TIP :
Provide a choice of nuts, dried fruit, and fresh seasonal fruit or stewed fruit so guests can pick a favorite.

CHOCOLATE CHIA PARFAITS

The perfect combination of creamy chocolate and wholesome chia seeds, these parfaits are great to make in advance if you're short on time, as they will last for up to a week in the refrigerator. Whether you're hosting a laid-back brunch with friends or treating yourself to a midmorning snack, these parfaits are sure to hit the spot.

SERVES : 4
PREP TIME : 10 MINS
CHILL TIME : 2 HOURS
TO OVERNIGHT

½ cup (85g) chia seeds
2 cups (500ml) milk (dairy
    or plant-based)
¼ cup (25g) unsweetened
    cocoa powder
¼ cup (60ml) maple syrup
1 teaspoon vanilla extract
¾ cup (200g) Greek yogurt
4 tablespoons Cacao Nut Crunch
    (page 206)

In a large mixing bowl, whisk the chia seeds, milk, cocoa, maple syrup, and vanilla together thoroughly until the cocoa is fully incorporated and there are no lumps. Let the mixture stand for 2 minutes, then whisk again to prevent clumping. Cover the bowl and refrigerate for at least 2 hours or overnight. This allows the chia seeds to absorb the liquid and form a pudding-like consistency.

Once the pudding has thickened, remove it from the refrigerator and stir to ensure it's well combined and smooth.

Take 4 serving glasses or jars and begin layering the parfaits. Start with a large spoonful of the chocolate chia pudding at the bottom of each glass. Next, add a layer of yogurt, then continue layering with alternating layers of chocolate chia pudding and yogurt until you reach the top of the glass, finishing with a final layer of yogurt. Top each parfait with a sprinkling of the crunchy nut topping.

LIGHT & FRESH

SUBS :
Use fresh berries or other fruits on hand as well as or instead of the crunch to top with.

BLUEBERRY CHIA PUDDINGS

This is another perfect make-ahead brunch recipe. Like the parfaits (page 36), these desserts will last for up to a week stored in the refrigerator. As it is so easy to substitute different fruits, toppings, and additions, they are great to add to a last minute brunch party table.

SERVES : 4
PREP TIME : 10 MINS
CHILL TIME : 2 HOURS
TO OVERNIGHT

1 cup (250ml) coconut milk
　(or any nut milk)
1 teaspoon vanilla bean paste
2 tablespoons maple syrup
⅓ cup (60g) chia seeds
1 cup (125g) fresh blueberries
2 tablespoons pumpkin seeds,
　for serving

In a medium bowl, whisk the coconut milk, vanilla, maple syrup, and chia seeds together until combined. Set aside for 5 minutes, then whisk again to make sure the chia are evenly dispersed. Add half of the fresh berries and gently mix through.

Transfer the pudding to small serving dishes or jars, cover, and refrigerate for 2 hours, or until set. Top with the remaining berries and the pumpkin seeds to serve.

TIP :
Style these puddings in a little teacups or a mixture of jars to match your party table setting and add a little fun. They can be all served together in the middle of the table on a cake stand to give some height and layers to the table.

SALTED CARAMEL BLISS BALLS

MAKES : 14
PREP TIME : 15 MINS
COOK TIME : 0 MINS

2 cups (150g) unsweetened
    shredded coconut
12 Medjool dates (220g), pitted
1½ tablespoons tahini paste
1 teaspoon vanilla extract
Large pinch of flaky sea salt
3 tablespoons toasted or plain
    sesame seeds, for coating.

These bliss balls are a great treat to have on hand, as they are a little sweet bite for in between meals. They are quick and easy to include in a brunch spread as they can be prepared ahead.

Add all the ingredients, except the sesame seeds, to a food processor and process until everything is combined and the mixture is a sandy texture. Using about 1 ounce (30g) of the mixture, press together and roll into small balls. Spread the sesame seeds out on a plate and roll each ball in the sesame seeds until coated, then repeat with the remaining balls. Store your bliss balls in an airtight container in the refrigerator for up to 2 weeks.

CHOC PEANUT BLISS BALLS

MAKES : 16
PREP TIME : 15 MINS
COOK TIME : 0 MINS

12 Medjool dates (220g), pitted
1 cup (90g) almond meal
½ cup (50g) rolled oats
¼ cup (20g) unsweetened cocoa
    powder
3 tablespoons peanut butter
1½ tablespoons honey
1 teaspoon vanilla extract
4 tablespoons unsweetened
    shredded coconut, for coating

Chocolate and peanut butter makes a delicious flavor combination. These are a great choice for everyone in my family.

Add all the ingredients, except the coconut, to a food processor and process for 1 minute, or until smooth and it has a breadcrumb-like, sandy consistency. Using about 1 ounce (30g) of the mixture, press together and roll into small balls. Spread the coconut out on a plate and roll each ball in the coconut until coated, then repeat with the remaining balls. Store your bliss balls in an airtight container in the refrigerator for up to 2 weeks.

TIP :
You can swap out ingredients for what you have on hand or to make a quick change depending on your cravings.

CHOCOLATE CHERRY BITES

These bites are a decadent treat, perfectly paired with a coffee to finish your brunch on a sweet note. They can be made a few days ahead and kept refrigerated until you need them.

MAKES : 15
PREP TIME : 20 MINS
CHILL TIME : 1 TO 3 HOURS

1 cup (165g) frozen cherries
½ cup (75g) frozen berries, such as strawberries, raspberries, blueberries
1½ cups (120g) unsweetened shredded coconut
2 tablespoons unsweetened cocoa powder
1 tablespoon maple syrup
1 teaspoon vanilla extract
7 ounces (200g) semisweet chocolate, chopped

Line an 8 by 4 inch (20 by 10cm) baking pan with baking parchment, making sure the parchment reaches up the sides of the pan.

Add the frozen cherries, frozen berries, shredded coconut, cocoa, maple syrup, and vanilla to a food processor and blend to a wet sandy-textured mix. Spoon the mixture into the prepared pan and, using the back of a spoon, press the mixture into the pan, smoothing and compressing it as you go. Once the surface is smooth and level, freeze for at least 1 hour or up to 3 hours. In a microwave-safe bowl, melt the chocolate in 30-second intervals, stirring between each interval until smooth.

Remove the cherry coconut mixture from the freezer, leave it in the pan, and carefully pour the melted dark chocolate over the top, spreading it out so that it completely covers the cherry coconut mixture. Chill in the refrigerator for 15 to 20 minutes until the chocolate hardens.

Use a hot sharp knife to cut the slice into small squares before the chocolate has fully set. Return the dish to the refrigerator to continue to set before serving. Alternatively, store in an airtight container in the refrigerator for up to 2 weeks.

TIP :
If you can't find frozen cherries, replace them with the same amount of canned cherries. Just be sure to drain the canned cherries well or the mixture will be too wet.

TOASTS & TOPPINGS

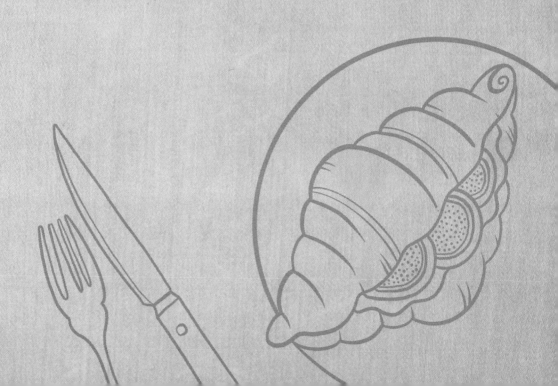

PEANUT BUTTER TOASTS WITH STRAWBERRIES & SESAME

There is nothing better than a sweet and salty combination. Try this simple nut butter toast and it might become your favorite too. The toast also looks beautiful topped with edible flowers if you have time to pick them up; chamomile is a perfect match.

SERVES : 4
PREP TIME : 5 MINS
COOK TIME : 0 MINS

4 thick slices sourdough bread
⅓ cup (85g) peanut butter
10 to 12 ripe strawberries, sliced
1 tablespoon toasted sesame seeds
2 teaspoons honey
Chamomile flowers, for garnish
   (optional)

Toast the bread and spread generously with the peanut butter. Layer the sliced strawberries on top and sprinkle with toasted sesame seeds and a drizzle of honey. Garnish with some chamomile flowers, if desired.

SUBS :
If some of your guests are vegan then replace the honey with maple syrup.
You can also use almond butter instead of peanut butter, if you prefer.

AVOCADO, BACON & TOMATO SOURDOUGH

SERVES : 4
PREP TIME : 5 MINS
COOK TIME : 20 MINS

4 slices streaky (lean) bacon
4 thick slices sourdough bread
2 tablespoons butter or olive oil
2 large ripe avocados, halved
    and pitted
Juice of 1 lime
1 large tomato, cut into 8 thin slices
Salt and black pepper

Preheat the oven to 400°F (200°C). Place the bacon on a baking sheet and bake in the oven for 10 minutes, then check how it is cooking. Depending on the thickness of your bacon it may only take a few more minutes. Once crispy and golden, transfer the bacon to a plate lined with paper towels.

If you have a hot plate or large pan, brush each slice of bread with oil or butter and toast on the pan for 2 minutes on each side. You can also use a regular toaster and then butter afterward. Meanwhile, scoop out 4 avocado halves. Carefully slice each half and squeeze with lime juice, ready to fan over each slice of toast.

Layer each toasted slice of sourdough with 2 tomato slices, a slice of the cooked bacon on top, then fan and flatten each sliced avocado half on top. Season well before serving.

PESTO, AVOCADO & FETA TOAST

SERVES : 4
PREP TIME : 5 MINS
COOK TIME : 5 MINS

2 to 3 ripe avocados
2 tablespoons lemon juice
7 ounces (200g) feta cheese,
    crumbled
1 tablespoon olive oil
3 tablespoons dukkah
4 thick slices sourdough bread
⅓ cup (80ml) Pesto (page 214)
Sea salt

Halve the avocados, remove the pits, and cut into coarse cubes. Place in a small bowl and pour the lemon juice over to coat. Add the feta, olive oil, and half of the dukkah and gently mix to combine.

Toast the sourdough, then spread the pesto evenly over the slices. Heap the avocado and feta mix on top of each toast and top with the remaining dukkah and a sprinkle of sea salt to taste.

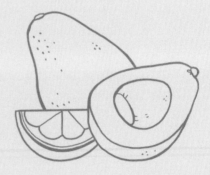

SMOKED SALMON WITH PICKLED ONIONS

(NF)

This is one of my all-time favorite flavor combinations on toast. It will go well on any bread, but dark rye adds a deep earthy flavor, which is extra special.

SERVES : 4
PREP TIME : 10 MINS
COOK TIME : 5 MINS

4 slices of rye bread
   (or pumpernickel)
⅔ cup (150g) cream cheese
4½ ounces (125g) smoked salmon
2 tablespoons baby capers
Black pepper
Juice of ½ lemon, plus wedges,
   for garnish
Quick Pickled Onions,
   for garnish (page 212)

Toast the bread slices, then top with a thick layer of cream cheese, smoked salmon, capers, a squeeze of lemon juice, and some pickled onions. Arrange on a large serving plate, season with pepper, and garnish with lemon wedges. Cover and keep refrigerated until ready to serve. It's a good idea to have some extras of all the ingredients on the table as guests may like to make another one.

SUBS :
- If you haven't made the pickled onions, fresh herbs such as dill, chives, or parsley are a good alternative or even an addition.
- Add a soft-boiled egg cut in half.

RICOTTA & FIG CROISSANTS

Because the croissants are toasted, they don't need to be fresh that day. The buttery texture of the toasted pastry will be delicious and melt in your mouth. You can serve with extra ricotta and figs to spread on the top half, if desired.

SERVES : 4
PREP TIME : 5 MINS
COOK TIME : 5 MINS

4 croissants
1 cup (225g) ricotta cheese, drained
2 tablespoons confectioners' sugar
1 tablespoon lemon juice
1 tablespoon finely grated lemon zest
4 figs, sliced, plus extra 2 figs, sliced, for serving
2 tablespoons honey

Slice the croissants in half to make an open sandwich.

In a small bowl, use a spoon to beat together the ricotta, confectioners' sugar, lemon juice, and zest. Spread the bottom layer of each croissant generously with the ricotta mixture and top with a sliced fig.

Preheat the broiler. Place the prepared croissants including the croissant tops on a large baking sheet and set under the broiler for 2 to 3 minutes. Broil the tops of the croissants for only 30 seconds to 1 minute. Watch them, as they toast very quickly. Drizzle the honey over the top of the warmed figs and serve with the toasted tops, remaining ricotta mixture, and the extra fig slices.

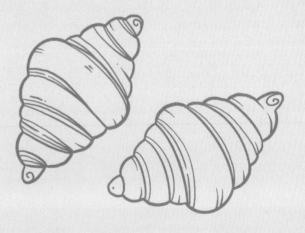

SUBS :
Other fruits to use include strawberries, baked rhubarb (page 19), thinly sliced pear with grated nutmeg, or stewed apple slices with cinnamon.

SWEET BLACKBERRY BAGEL

The simplest toppings on fresh bagels are always the best. If you can buy fresh there's no need to even toast the bagels for this recipe. The sweet, creamy mixture pairs deliciously with the burst from the berries. Mixing the filling together in a bowl saves time when making larger numbers—you can easily double or triple this recipe if you have lots of hungry guests.

SERVES : 4
PREP TIME : 5 MINS
COOK TIME : 5 MINS

4 plain bagels
2 tablespoons slivered almonds
½ cup (60g) confectioners' sugar
1 cup (225g) cream cheese
1 cup (150g) fresh blackberries

Cut and toast the bagels.

Heat a small nonstick skillet over medium heat and toast the almonds for 3 to 4 minutes, shaking the pan as you cook. You will smell their fragrance and see the color turning brown. Don't leave them unattended, as they burn quickly.

Meanwhile, sift the confectioners' sugar and combine in a food processor with the cream cheese. Process until the cream cheese mixture is smooth. Add the blackberries and give one more pulse to chop and mix through.

Spread the cream cheese mixture over the toasted bagel bases, then top with the toasted almonds and the bagel tops.

EGG SALAD BAGEL

If you don't have a good bagel store nearby, it's easy to have some always on hand in the freezer. I prefer to toast bagels once they've been in the freezer, as it helps to bring the freshness back. Pop them straight into the toaster and use the defrost setting. Make these and another bagel recipe (page 56) so all your guests can have a half of each kind. I find it too hard to choose between the sweet and savory.

SERVES : 4
PREP TIME : 5 MINS
COOK TIME : 10 MINS

6 large eggs
2 scallions, halved and thinly sliced
1 large handful of dill, chopped
1 tablespoon Dijon mustard
3 tablespoons mayonnaise
4 bagels of choice
2 tablespoons butter
3 ounces (85g) snow pea or alfalfa
   sprouts
Sea salt and black pepper

Bring a small saucepan of water to a boil. Once the water is boiling, use a spoon to carefully lower in each egg. Boil the eggs for 7 minutes before removing and running under cool water to stop the cooking process. Peel the eggs and add to a mixing bowl with the scallions, dill, mustard, and mayonnaise. Using a fork, mash the eggs and mix together until everything is combined. Season well with salt and pepper.

Depending on the freshness of the bagels, you can just slice them in half, or if frozen, toast the bagels and spread both sides with butter. Layer the base of each bagel with 2 large spoonfuls of the egg mix, then top with the sprouts and the top half of the bagels. Slice in half before serving.

TOASTS & TOPPINGS

SWEET TOASTS

Set up a table with tea or coffee and a host of options for guests to make their own toasts. Buy good-quality breads and pastries and use little jars and bowls to display a selection of delicious toppings. Here are some ideas for a sweet, fruity toast spread.

SWEET TOAST FEAST

SERVES : 8
PREP TIME : 20 MINS
COOK TIME : 40 MINS

COCONUT CREAM :
1 (15-ounce / 425g) can full-fat
   coconut cream (refrigerate the
   night before use)
¼ cup (40g) confectioners' sugar,
   sifted, plus extra for dusting
½ teaspoon vanilla extract or ½
   vanilla bean, seeds scraped out

BAKED RICOTTA :
Scant 1 cup (200g) soft ricotta
   cheese
2 tablespoons superfine sugar
Finely grated zest of 1 orange,
   setting aside a little for the top
½ teaspoon ground cinnamon

HONEY AND BRIE :
7-ounce (200g) round Brie cheese
1 square of wild raw honeycomb
2 to 3 figs, halved or quartered
2 to 4 slices sourdough bread,
   halved

FOR ASSEMBLY :
2 bagels, halved
4 pastries, croissants, or brioche
   rolls
1 (16-ounce / 450g) jar compote
   or curd (store-bought or try the
   recipes on page 209)
Toasted coconut flakes, for garnish
1½ cups (200g) mixed fresh berries
2 to 3 bananas
1 (16-ounce / 450g) jar nut butter
4½ ounces (125g) dark chocolate,
   finely chopped or grated
½ cup (50g) Cacao Nut Crunch
   (page 206)

Use a combination of pantry staple spreads with sliced fresh fruit and a few flavor sprinkles to create a feast of sweet toasts.

COCONUT CREAM :
After refrigerating the coconut cream overnight, scrape out all of the solidified cream into a bowl. Set aside any liquid for use later. Use electric beaters to whisk the cream for 30 seconds. Add the sugar and vanilla and beat for 1 minute, or until creamy and smooth with light peaks. Use at once or chill for 1 to 2 weeks.

BAKED RICOTTA :
Drain the ricotta well if not pot set. Preheat the oven to 375°F (190°C). Mix the ricotta with the superfine sugar, orange zest, and cinnamon in a bowl. Spoon the ricotta mixture into a 1-cup (250ml) capacity ramekin and smooth the top. Bake for 30 minutes. Serve with confectioners' sugar and more orange zest.

HONEY AND BRIE :
Serving honey in its raw honeycomb form will add a little wow factor to your platter. Slightly warm your Brie cheese in the oven or microwave, top with a honeycomb square, and serve with torn figs. (Fresh or dried on the vine grapes are a good alternative, too.)

TO ASSEMBLE :
Spread the chosen bread or pastry base with compote, top with coconut cream, and sprinkle with coconut flakes. Serve with the honey and Brie, berries, bananas, nut butter, grated chocolate, and nut crunch.

SUGGESTED TOPPING COMBOS :
· Nut butter, sliced banana, drizzle of honey, and shaved dark chocolate
· Baked ricotta and strawberries
· Brie, honey, and a sweet nut topping
· Berry compote, coconut cream, and toasted coconut flakes

TOASTS & TOPPINGS

SAVORY TOAST FEAST

SERVES : 8
PREP TIME : 20 MINS
COOK TIME : 20 MINS

Use these simple recipe ideas to create a delicious spread of savory toast topping options.

CONFIT CHERRY TOMATOES :
8 ounces (225g) cherry tomatoes, halved
2 tablespoons olive oil
2 teaspoons balsamic vinegar

WHIPPED FETA DIP :
7-ounce (200g) block feta cheese
3 tablespoons cream cheese
½ tablespoon finely grated lemon zest
2 tablespoons lemon juice

FOR ASSEMBLY :
4 thick slices sourdough bread, toasted and halved
4 bagels, halved and toasted
6 slices turkey meat
6 slices Danish salami
6 slices Swiss cheese
2 handfuls of arugula leaves
1 to 2 avocados, sliced
2 medium to large tomatoes, sliced
1 (16-ounce / 450g) jar Tomato Chili Relish (page 214)
1 (10-ounce / 280g) jar Fennel Quick Pickle (make using the recipe on page 212, swapping out the onion for 1 head of shaved fennel and a good handful of the fennel fronds, then add 1 tablespoon of yellow mustard seeds)
½ cup (65g) Tamari Seed Mix (page 206) or buy some Everything Bagel Seasoning
Butter or olive oil, for spreading
Flaky sea salt and black pepper

CONFIT CHERRY TOMATOES :
Preheat the oven to 375°F (190°C). Place the cherry tomatoes in a baking pan and drizzle with olive oil and a good sprinkling of sea salt. Bake for about 15 minutes. The tomatoes will have softened and started to brown on top. Give them a gentle stir and pour over the balsamic vinegar. Return to the oven for 2 to 3 minutes if the tomatoes need any further cooking. Let cool slightly before adding a few spoonfuls over the whipped feta dip. Store the remaining tomatoes and oil in an airtight container in the refrigerator.

WHIPPED FETA DIP :
I like to make this simple dip and top with the confit cherry tomatoes above. It's a little wow centerpiece for your toasts table and can be used with all of the other toppings to create yummy toast toppings. Add both cheeses, lemon zest, and lemon juice to a food processor and blend until the cheeses are combined, creamy, and smooth. Spoon out into a shallow bowl and top with the warm confit cherry tomatoes.

TO ASSEMBLE :
Arrange the breads, different meats, sliced cheese, and arugula on a large serving board, then add the avocados and tomatoes to a shallow bowl, and surround with the dip, relish, pickles, and seed topping. Make sure there is butter or olive oil and seasoning.

PRESENTATION TIPS :
Use large platters, wooden boards, and small bowls to layer and create a pretty centerpiece to your table. Think about serving utensils and spoons for guests to use on each item on the table.

SUGGESTED TOPPING COMBOS :
- Avocado, salami, pickled fennel
- Arugula, whipped feta, and confit cherry tomatoes with tamari seed topping
- Tomato relish, Swiss cheese, and turkey
- Tomato slices, pickled fennel, and tamari seed topping

SAVORY TOASTS

Here are some ideas for a savory toast spread. You could have all the breads toasted or you can set up the toaster on the table for a toast-your-own situation. Your guests will enjoy trying a few different topping options and being able to help themselves.

PESTO HALLOUMI STACK

We're using roasted sweet potato as our toast for this recipe. It adds a little restaurant quality touch but it's still as easy as adding a tasty topping to a toast.

SERVES : 4
PREP TIME : 10 MINS
COOK TIME : 30 MINS

2 medium sweet potatoes,
    skin scrubbed and cut in half
    lengthwise
2 large yellow bell peppers, seeded
    and cut into wide strips
1 small red onion, quartered
3 tablespoons olive oil
1 medium zucchini
1 lemon
8 ounces (225g) halloumi cheese,
    cut into ½-inch (1cm) thick slices
⅓ cup (60g) Pesto (page 214
    or store-bought)
1 large handful of baby spinach
    or arugula leaves, plus extra
    for serving
Sea salt and black pepper

Preheat the oven to 375°F (190°C). Line a large baking sheet with baking parchment and spread out the sweet potatoes, pepper strips, and quartered onion. Drizzle 2 tablespoons of the olive oil over the vegetables and season well. Roast in the oven for 20–25 minutes. Remove the onion and peppers once they are charred and softened (check after 15 minutes). The sweet potato should be soft when pierced with a fork but still holding its shape.

Meanwhile, use a vegetable peeler to peel long, thin strips of zucchini. Coat the zucchini strips in the remaining olive oil, a squeeze of lemon juice, and a sprinkle of salt. Heat a medium skillet or griddle pan and fry the halloumi over medium heat for 3 to 4 minutes on each side, or until golden brown. Fry the zucchini strips for just 1 minute on each side.

BUILD YOUR STACK :
Spread the pesto over each sweet potato half. Top with the spinach, a red onion quarter, halloumi, pepper strips, and top with curls of the fried zucchini. Season to taste with salt and pepper and serve with lemon cheeks and extra spinach.

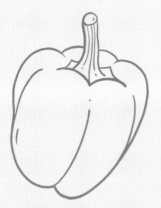

SUBS :
- Make this stack on a bagel or sourdough instead of the sweet potato.
- Swap the halloumi for bacon if you have pork-loving guests.
- Replace the halloumi with avocado slices if you have a vegan guest.
- Adding an egg is never a bad option at a brunch too.

QUICK FETA
EGG TORTILLA

You might need to double the ingredients for these. They are really quick and easy to make, but they are so tasty, you may have immediate orders for seconds!

SERVES : 4
PREP TIME : 5 MINS
COOK TIME : 15 MINS

5½ ounces (150g) feta cheese

4 eggs

1 teaspoon sea salt

1 teaspoon red pepper flakes

4 (4½-inch / 11.5cm) flour tortillas (soft tacos)

1 avocado, peeled, pitted, and sliced

6 to 8 cherry tomatoes, halved

½ cup (15g) cilantro leaves

2 tablespoons Quick Pickled Onions (page 212)

If you have a large skillet, you can make a few of these at the same time. Use a pan that has a lid. Heat the pan over medium to high heat. Crumble a quarter of the feta in a 4-inch (10cm) circle (just under the size of your tortilla) into the pan. Make as many feta circles as you can fit into your pan. As the feta begins to cook and melt, crack an egg into the center of each circle. Sprinkle each egg with ¼ teaspoon of salt and ¼ teaspoon of pepper flakes. Cover the pan with a lid.

Lay your tortillas out on a large plate with a couple of slices of avocado on top. Once the egg is cooked and the cheese around the edge has crisped up, divide among the tortillas. Top with a little more avocado, some cherry tomato halves, cilantro leaves, and pickled onions.

Let cool for a few minutes before serving. Instruct guests to pick up and eat like a taco if they can. The egg yolk will break and form a delicious sauce for the rest of the ingredients.

FRIED EGG &
KALE SANDWICH

I like to cook my eggs so the yolk is runny, so as it mixes with the
relish and kale in this sandwich it creates a tasty brunch bite.
You can swap out the muffin for a brioche or potato bun, if desired.

SERVES : 4
PREP TIME : 5 MINS
COOK TIME : 10 MINS

1 tablespoon olive oil

1 garlic clove

2 curly kale stalks, stems removed
   and leaves torn

⅓ cup (80ml) chicken stock

2 tablespoons butter, plus extra
   for greasing

4 medium eggs

4 English muffins, sliced in half

2 tablespoons Tomato Chili Relish
   (page 214)

Sea salt

Heat the olive oil in a skillet with a lid. Smash the garlic and add to
the oil to flavor. Add the kale leaves to the pan and sauté for 1 to 2
minutes before pouring the stock over and covering the pan with
the lid. Let the kale braise for 3 to 4 minutes, then remove from the
heat and set aside.

    If you have them, grease 4 egg rings with butter to keep your
eggs the same size as the English muffins and add to the skillet.
Crack the eggs into the rings or straight into the pan. Season with
salt and flip over easy for a minute before removing from the heat.
Toast the muffins, butter, and spread with relish. Fill each muffin
with the braised kale leaves and an egg.

SUBS :
If you don't have any tomato relish on hand, then use your favorite hot sauce
instead. To make this vegetarian use water instead of the chicken stock.

SAUSAGE & EGG BREAKFAST BURGER

This is a restaurant-quality breakfast burger with a few tricks to speed up the prep. Baking the eggs gives you some time to get the rest of the burger ready to go. If you're not a hot sauce person, swap it out for the more subtle Tomato Chili Relish on page 214.

SERVES : 4
PREP TIME : 10 MINS
COOK TIME : 20 MINS

Butter, for greasing
5 eggs
½ cup (120ml) milk
¾ cup (85g) grated Gouda cheese
½ pound (225g) ground pork
4 burger buns
¼ cup (60g) mayonnaise
¼ cup (60g) hot sauce
1 large handful of arugula leaves
Salt and black pepper

Preheat the oven to 350°F (180°C). Grease a 6 by 6-inch (15 by 15cm) baking dish with butter. In a medium bowl, whisk the eggs, milk, grated cheese, and seasoning together. Pour the egg mix into the prepared pan and bake for 15 minutes, or until set when you wobble the pan. About halfway through cooking, stir the eggs briefly with a fork and transfer the pan to the oven.

Meanwhile, heat a medium skillet over medium to high heat. Divide the ground pork into 4 portions and shape into balls. One at a time, press the balls of meat flat into the pan, then sprinkle with salt and cook for 3 to 4 minutes before flipping to cook the other side. Repeat for each ball.

Toast the buns under the broiler or in a toaster and spread the base of the buns with 1 tablespoon of the mayonnaise and hot sauce, and a few arugula leaves.

Once the egg has cooked, cool for 2 minutes, then remove from the pan and cut into 4 even squares. Stack the cooked sausage patty and egg squares onto the prepared burger bases. Add the toasted bun top and serve.

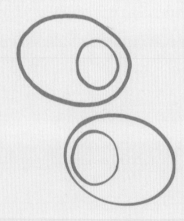

73

GRILLED PEACH & BURRATA FLATBREAD

Burrata is a delicate, yet thick and creamy cow's milk cheese. The simplest pairings stand out but this combination of sweet warm peaches and basil will have your taste buds dancing.

SERVES : 4
PREP TIME : 5 TO 10 MINS
COOK TIME : 10 MINS

1 tablespoon olive oil

4 flatbreads or pita pockets
    or try the recipe on page 142

2 peaches, pitted and cut into
    wedges

2 (8-ounce / 225g) burrata balls,
    torn

2 handfuls of basil leaves

1 tablespoon balsamic glaze

Sea salt

Heat a griddle pan or flat grill plate. Add the olive oil in small batches as you heat, to coat the pan. If using the dough recipe to make your own flatbread, roll out 4 thin circles of the dough and grill for a few minutes on each side. The dough will puff up as it cooks. If using store-bought flatbread, then toast on the grill plate to warm.

Place the peaches, flesh-side down, on the griddle pan or grill plate and cook for 1 to 2 minutes on each side. Season with sea salt as the peaches cook.

Spread the warm flatbreads with torn burrata and top with basil leaves and the warm peach wedges. Add a drizzle of balsamic glaze before serving.

TIP :
Add prosciutto to this dish for a salty boost.

TOASTED MORTADELLA FOCACCIA

NF

If you can't find a good focaccia bread you can also make this with ciabatta rolls. Mortadella doesn't need much to help it shine, so keep it simple with these.

SERVES : 4
PREP TIME : 10 MINS
COOK TIME : 10 MINS

4 squares focaccia
8 ounces (225g) mortadella slices
2 ripe tomatoes, sliced
2 (8-ounce / 225g) mozzarella balls, sliced
1 flat leaf parsley sprig, leaves coarsely chopped
Butter or olive oil (optional)
Salt and black pepper

Slice the focaccia into 2 halves. Layer the mortadella, tomatoes, and mozzarella onto the bottom halves, then season well. Sprinkle with chopped parsley and season well again. Place the top half of the focaccia on top and sandwich together. Heat a large skillet or grill plate and spread or brush the bread top and bottom with butter or oil, then toast each side of the focaccia for 3 to 4 minutes. Press down with a weight in between to make sure the heat gets through to melt the mozzarella. Slice in half and serve warm.

TIP :
If you have a sandwich press, use this to toast the sandwiches, or you can toast them under a preheated broiler.

GRILLED SMOKED CHEESE FOCACCIA

(NF)

The smoky flavor of the cheese mixed with the sweet tomato chili relish is a winning combination.

SERVES : 4
PREP TIME : 5 MINS
COOK TIME : 5 MINS

1 slab focaccia
Butter, for spreading
¼ cup (60g) Tomato Chili Relish
    (page 214 or store-bought)
2 handfuls of arugula leaves
6 ounces (175g) leg of ham, sliced
    off the bone
4½ ounces (125g) smoked Cheddar
    cheese, sliced or grated
Salt and black pepper

Preheat the broiler. Cut the focaccia into large squares and slice through the middle to open them up. Spread the bottom half of the bread with butter and top with the tomato relish. Layer some arugula, ham slices, and cheese on top. Season and place together on a baking sheet. Broil for 4 to 5 minutes until the cheese is nicely melted and browning. Serve immediately.

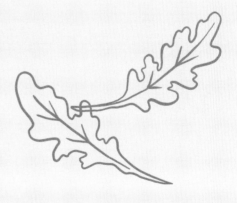

SUBS :
Use 2 large ciabatta rolls instead of the focaccia, if desired. For a vegetarian version, simply omit the sliced ham and make sure the smoked cheese is suitable for vegetarians.

PLATTERS
& BOWLS

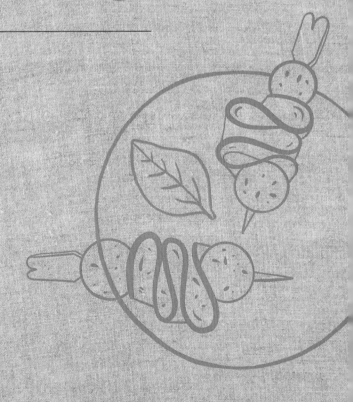

GRANOLA PORRIDGE WITH QUICK POACHED PLUMS

Using a premade granola to make this warm oatmeal recipe adds texture and flavor without any extra work. Granola is an item I always keep stocked in my pantry so it's easy to whip this up in no time.

SERVES : 4
PREP TIME : 5 MINS
COOK TIME : 15 MINS

12 ounces (3 large) plums
1 tablespoon maple syrup
   or superfine sugar
2 cups (240g) Granola, (page 205)
2 cups (500ml) milk
2 tablespoons ground flaxseed
⅔ cup (150g) plain yogurt

Halve, pit, and slice the plums into wedges, about 8 per plum. Heat a medium pan over low heat, add the plums, maple syrup, and ½ tablespoon of water, and poach for 7 to 8 minutes, stirring occasionally to make sure each side of the plum wedge is cooked and coated in the syrup. Remove from the heat when the fruit has softened and the syrupy liquid has reduced.

In a separate pan, combine the granola, 1½ cups (370ml) water, and 1 cup (250ml) of the milk. Heat over low heat for 8 to 10 minutes, stirring every couple of minutes, making sure the milk doesn't fully come to a boil. The granola will absorb the milk and the mixture will thicken. Depending on the ratio of oats in your granola you may need to add more milk. I like a thicker, dry texture to my oatmeal, but if you prefer it creamier then add all the remaining milk and stir through to combine.

Serve with a sprinkling of flaxseed, a dollop of yogurt, and the poached plums.

SUBS :
- Use any milk of your choice, plant or animal-based. It's also fine to use just water, if preferred.
- If you don't have any fresh fruit, add a few tablespoons of compote when you serve the oatmeal. Try the recipe on page 209.

BANANA CHIA QUINOA

This warm, pudding-like dish is so comforting. It can be served directly from the pan at the table or if you have a little time serve individually with a mixture of fresh fruits.

SERVES : 4
PREP TIME : 5 MINS
COOK TIME : 10 MINS

1 cup (120g) quinoa flakes
¼ cup (40g) black chia seeds,
    plus extra for decorating
1 teaspoon ground cinnamon
1 cup (250ml) milk of choice,
    plus extra for serving
3 bananas
Honey, for serving

Combine the quinoa, chia seeds, cinnamon, 1½ cups (375ml) water, and half of the milk in a medium saucepan and cook, stirring, over low heat for 7 to 8 minutes. As the liquid is absorbed, add more of the remaining milk.

While cooking, mash 2 of the bananas in a bowl. Slice the remaining banana for the decoration and set aside. Once the chia mixture is a creamy consistency, turn off the heat and fold through the mashed banana. Serve with a sprinkling of extra chia seeds, the reserved banana slices, and a drizzle of honey.

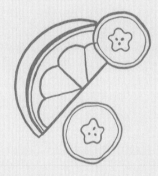

TIP :
If you don't have any milk, use water and fold through a spoonful of yogurt before serving.

SUBS :
- Bananas are a regular in our household as I always have them on hand, but you can swap them for freezer berries, chopped dried fruit (add those at the beginning of cooking), or poached fruit, if desired.
- Replace the quinoa flakes with rolled oats.

MANGO COCONUT RICE PUDDING

This rice pudding is so simple. You can eat it warm, or cold as it's traditionally eaten. It's sweet and delicious at any time of the day.

SERVES : 6
PREP TIME : 5 MINS
COOK TIME : 35 MINS

1 cup (220g) arborio rice
4 cups (1L) milk of choice
⅓ cup (60g) superfine sugar
Pinch of sea salt
½ cup (125ml) coconut milk
1 teaspoon vanilla extract

FOR SERVING :

2 mangoes, peeled and sliced
  or diced
3 tablespoons toasted shredded
  coconut, for decorating

In a medium saucepan, combine the rice, milk, sugar, and salt. Bring to a boil, stirring occasionally. Be careful not to walk away as the milk will boil over if left. Once it's just about to boil, turn the heat down to a low simmer, cover with a lid, and cook for 25 minutes. Check the rice, add half of the coconut milk, and cook, stirring, for another 5 minutes as the remaining milk is absorbed. Add the vanilla and stir through. If you're serving it cold, transfer to a serving dish and cover with plastic wrap, pressing the wrap down on the surface of the rice to prevent a skin forming. Refrigerate until ready to serve.

When ready to serve, if the pudding has been refrigerated, then use the remaining half of the coconut milk to stir through to soften and loosen to your preferred consistency. Top with the mango and toasted coconut.

MAKE AHEAD :
Make this a day in advance, store in the refrigerator, then it's ready to go in a couple of minutes.

SUBS :
· Try this with different fruits and crunchy toppings, such as raisins and slivered almonds, diced plums, and pistachios.
· Swap the coconut milk for cream to keep it more classic.
· For a vegan dish, substitute the milk for a plant-based option.

SOFT SCRAMBLE EGGS WITH LABNEH

Cooking eggs to order at a party can be rather time consuming and difficult with different guests' taste preferences, so use this soft scramble recipe. It is so delicate and flavorful and very quick to whip up. Everyone will love it.

SERVES : 4
PREP TIME : 5 MINS
COOK TIME : 10 MINS

8 large eggs
1 teaspoon sea salt
1 tablespoon olive oil
⅓ cup (80ml) labneh, plus extra
    for serving
Salt and black pepper

FOR SERVING :
Olive oil
2 tablespoons chopped herbs, such
    as dill, chives, or flat-leaf parsley
Toast

Whisk the eggs, salt, and half of the olive oil together in a medium bowl until combined.

Heat a large nonstick skillet over medium heat and add the remaining olive oil. Pour the whisked eggs into the pan and cook for 8 to 10 minutes, using a rubber spatula to stir the eggs gently as they cook. Once the eggs are beginning to set (there should still be some wet patches on top), turn off the heat and add the labneh. Gently fold through the eggs so it is fully incorporated and the eggs have set. Season to taste with salt and pepper and serve.

A NOTE ON PRESENTATION :
This looks great served in a large serving bowl for guests to help themselves. Top with an extra scoop of labneh, a drizzle of oil, and chopped herbs with hot toast alongside.

SUBS :
Labneh is a thickened yogurt cheese, but if you can't buy any you can substitute with Greek yogurt or even a soft white cheese such as goat or cream cheese.

SHAKSHUKA EGGS

This simple one-pan dish will always impress. Nothing beats the hearty combination of subtly spiced tomato sauce with creamy, perfectly cooked eggs. It's delicious topped with fresh herbs and served with crusty bread to soak up all the saucy goodness.

SERVES : 4
PREP TIME : 5 MINS
COOK TIME : 30 MINS

2 tablespoons olive oil
1 onion, finely diced
3 garlic cloves, minced
1 red bell pepper, diced
1 teaspoon ground cumin
1 teaspoon paprika
½ teaspoon dried oregano
1 (15-ounce / 425g) can diced
    tomatoes
¼ teaspoon salt, or to taste
4 eggs
Black pepper

FOR THE GARNISH :
1½ ounces (40g) feta cheese,
    crumbled
1 handful of flat-leaf parsley

Heat the olive oil in a large skillet with a lid over medium heat. Add the onion and cook for 5 to 6 minutes until translucent, then add the garlic and bell pepper and cook until the pepper is softened. Stir in the spices and oregano and cook for 1 minute until fragrant.

Add the diced tomatoes, then add the salt and pepper to taste. Let the mixture simmer for 10 to 15 minutes until it thickens. The sauce needs to be thick enough to support the eggs as they cook.

Using a spoon, create 4 small wells evenly spaced in the tomato mixture (if the wells don't hold shape you may need to simmer the sauce a little longer to let it thicken). Carefully crack an egg into each well, trying to keep the egg contained in the well. Cover the skillet with a lid and let the eggs cook to your desired doneness, about 5 minutes for runny yolks.

Garnish with crumbled feta and parsley and serve straight from the skillet.

MAKE AHEAD :
To save time, the sauce can be made in advance and stored in the refrigerator until you are ready to serve. Simply reheat it in a large skillet and once it has come to a simmer continue with the rest of the recipe.

SUBS :
Fresh herbs or baby spinach are a great addition to this dish, or add some canned chickpeas or other beans at the same time as the canned tomatoes for extra flavor and texture.

WARM LENTIL BOWL WITH EGG

Lentils are a pantry staple of mine; they have an earthy nutty flavor that I love. This is a hearty brunch dish, especially on a cooler fall day. You can have the lentil mix already made and in the refrigerator, then just reheat and add fresh herbs, feta, and eggs.

SERVES : 4
PREP TIME : 10 MINS
COOK TIME : 40 MINS

¼ cup (60ml) olive oil, plus extra
    ½ tablespoon for frying the eggs
1 medium red onion, finely diced
4 garlic cloves, minced
½ tablespoon ground cumin
1 large carrot, diced
2 celery stalks, diced
2 Roma tomatoes, diced
1½ cups (300g) Puy lentils
2 cups (450ml) vegetable stock
    or water
1 tablespoon red wine vinegar
4 medium eggs
1 tablespoon hot pepper flakes
    (optional)
3½ cups (125g) watercress
1 handful of flat-leaf parsley,
    chopped
Sea salt and black pepper

Heat 2 tablespoons of the olive oil in a medium saucepan and gently sauté the onion for 5 to 6 minutes. Add the garlic and cumin and fry for 1 to 2 minutes before adding the diced vegetables, lentils, and stock. Bring to a boil, then season to taste with salt and pepper. Reduce the heat, cover with a lid, and simmer for about 25 minutes. The liquid should have been absorbed and the lentils softened and cooked. Remove from the heat and stir in the remaining oil and the vinegar. Season again. Cover and let cool slightly (at this point you could also cool and refrigerate it until you are planning to use).

Heat the extra ½ tablespoon of oil in a large skillet over medium heat and fry the eggs to your liking. Season with salt and hot pepper flakes, if using.

Fold the watercress through the warm lentil mixture. Top with the fried eggs and chopped parsley before serving.

SUBS :
· Add some grated Parmesan or feta if you're a cheese lover.
· To add extra protein and flavor, add 4 ounces (115g) diced speck when you are cooking the onions.

NORDIC BRUNCH
BOARD

A grazing spread is one of my favorite ways to eat meals with friends. It's visually stunning to see all the delicious food laid out on the table and as a host, all of your work is done. Sit down and enjoy the time and food with your guests.

NORDIC BRUNCH BOARD

SERVES : 6
PREP TIME : 20 MINS
COOK TIME : 10 MINS

SMOKED SALMON :

1 pound (450g) smoked salmon,
   sliced
1 lemon
3 tablespoons capers, for over
   the salmon, plus a small bowl
3 dill sprigs, plus 1 tablespoon for
   salmon and extra for garnish

CREAM CHEESE :

1 cup (225g) cream cheese
1 tablespoon milk
1 tablespoon chopped chives
1 (2-ounce / 55g) jar black lumpfish
   caviar

SOFT-BOILED EGGS :

6 eggs

FOR ASSEMBLY :

Small bowl of Quick Pickled Onions
   (page 212)
Fresh vegetables for colour
   and dipping—a mixture of
   sliced, halved, and whole can
   look visually appealing. Use
   cucumber, breakfast radish,
   heirloom large tomatoes
Selection of rye toasts and
   crispbread
3 to 4 bagels, halved
Flaky sea salt and black pepper

DRESS YOUR SALMON :

Separate each slice of smoked salmon so that they can be easily picked up by guests. Halve a lemon lengthwise and squeeze one half over the salmon. Cut the remaining half into wedges and scatter around the salmon for guests to add more if they choose. Top the salmon with 1 tablespoon of capers and 1 tablespoon of dill leaves and some flaky sea salt.

WHISK YOUR CREAM CHEESE :

You can easily create your own spreadable cream cheese, using a stand mixer or food processor. Beat the cream cheese until smooth and creamy, add the milk and chives and a g ood sprinkle of sea salt, and continue to beat until combined. Transfer to a small bowl for dipping and top with a spoonful of caviar for an extra touch.

PERFECT SOFT-BOILED EGGS :

Boil the perfect soft eggs with this method. Bring a medium saucepan of water to a boil. Once boiling, carefully lower the eggs into the water and set a timer for 6 minutes for soft-boiled eggs, 5 minutes, for runny or dippy eggs, and 8 minutes, for hard-boiled eggs. While the eggs are cooking, prepare a bowl of ice-cold water. After the timer goes, transfer the eggs to the ice bath to cool for at least 3 minutes.

For the brunch board, soft-boil your eggs, peel, and slice open. Serve with a good seasoning of flaky sea salt and black pepper.

TO ASSEMBLE :

Use a combination of large platters, bowls, and wooden boards to arrange the chopped vegetables, breads, and extra topping additions on the table. Pick a few extra drinks and sweet bites or desserts and your party is ready. Add them to the table as well and you can just enjoy. My picks from this book are: Classic Mimosa (page 178) and Yogurt pots with Rhubarb (page 19), or fresh berries and cinnamon. Don't forget to include some salt and pepper for guests to use, and arrange your napkins, plates, cutlery, and glassware, etc. as decoration. Doing it all beforehand helps to create the scene, and then once it's set there's nothing else you'll need to do.

SUBS :

You can try a variety of herbs, or roasted garlic, 1 to 2 teaspoons of horseradish or mustard as alternative add-ins.

ITALIAN BRUNCH BOARD

SERVES : 6
PREP TIME : 25 MINS
COOK TIME : 5 MINS

ZUCCHINI SKEWERS :

2 zucchini

1 tablespoon pesto, plus
    1 (10-ounce / 280g) jar for table

Olive oil

1 mint sprig, finely chopped

16 baby bocconcini balls

OLIVES :

6 strips unwaxed orange peel

2 garlic cloves

1 rosemary sprig

1 (4½-ounce / 125g) jar Sicilian
    green olives

14 ounces (400g) mixed tomatoes

BURRATA :

8-ounce (225g) burrata ball

1 bunch of basil

FOR ASSEMBLY :

Selection of cold cuts, such as
    mortadella, salami, prosciutto

1 (4½-ounce / 125g) box of grissini

Selection of sourdough slices,
    and/or focaccia

Fresh fruit such as purple grapes,
    figs, cantaloupe melon (wrap
    in prosciutto, see page 28)

1 or 2 small bowls of cornichons,
    roasted peppers, or artichokes

Balsamic vinegar

Salt and black pepper

ZUCCHINI SKEWERS (MAKES 12 TO 16) :

Use a vegetable peeler to peel long, thin strips of zucchini. In a shallow bowl, cover the zucchini with pesto, ½ tablespoon of olive oil, and the mint. If the zucchini is thin enough, this is nice left fresh; you can also give it a quick sear on a griddle pan but don't cook for too long or the zucchini will become soft and soggy. Add the bocconcini balls to the bowl and season well with salt and pepper. Thread the zucchini and bocconcini onto toothpicks or small bamboo skewers.

FOR THE OLIVES :

Heat ¼ cup (60ml) olive oil in a small pan and add the orange peel, garlic, and rosemary. Simmer for 5 minutes to let the flavors infuse the oil. Remove from the heat and let cool. After 10 minutes, while the oil is still warm, add the drained green olives and let cool to room temperature together. Serve in a small dish.

FOR THE BURRATA :

Cut the tomatoes in a variety of shapes and sizes and sprinkle with flaky sea salt. Add to a shallow serving dish. Tear the burrata into quarters and lay on top of the tomatoes. Season well with salt and pepper and a good drizzle of olive oil. Tear a handful of basil leaves over the top of the dish.

TO ASSEMBLE :

If you have a bread basket and some interesting serving bowls and plates, use these to create a visually appealing display of the breads and food for guests to help themselves from. Grouping similar ingredients together on on plates then adding extra layers around works well. If you can, use different kitchen items to create some height layers. A plate on top of an upturned bowl looks effective. As well as salt and pepper on the table fill a small dish with olive oil and top with balsamic vinegar, 2 parts oil to 1 part vinegar, so guests can use to dip their bread or add to the tomatoes.

ADDITIONS :

Add extra dishes and drinks to give your guests an even greater selection: Herby Fig Salad (page 30), Cherry Chocolate Bites (page 44), and Bailey's Cream Affogato (page 199).

ITALIAN BRUNCH
BOARD

An antipasto board will be a winner for me at any time of the day.
Combine a selection of cold cuts and simple ingredients to create
a delicious feast for your guests.

KIMCHI & MUSHROOM FRIED RICE

This fried rice is packed with flavor and can be whipped up in 10 minutes. It's best if you use precooked rice and have all the ingredients prepared ahead as you want to cook over high heat and keep the rice moving in the pan as much as possible.

SERVES : 4
PREP TIME : 15 MINS
COOK TIME : 20 MINS

2 tablespoons vegetable oil

1 onion, finely chopped

2 garlic cloves, minced

1 cup (100g) sliced mixed mushrooms, such as shiitake, cremini, or oyster

2 cups (300g) chopped greens, such as baby bok choy, Chinese broccoli, or spinach

2 cups (400g) cooked short-grain rice (preferably cooked the day before and kept in the refrigerator)

1 cup (150g) kimchi, chopped

4 eggs, beaten

FOR THE SAUCE :

4 tablespoons soy sauce

2 tablespoons gochujang

2 tablespoons sesame oil

FOR THE GARNISH :

2 scallions, thinly sliced

Black sesame seeds

For the sauce, in a small bowl, mix the soy sauce, gochujang, sesame oil, and 2 tablespoons of water together to create a sauce. Set aside.

Heat the vegetable oil in a large skillet or wok over medium to high heat. Add the onion and garlic and cook for 5 to 6 minutes until the onion is translucent and the garlic is fragrant. Add the sliced mushrooms and cook for 3 to 4 minutes until the mushrooms are tender and golden brown. Stir in the greens, then add the cooked rice and break up any clumps. Stir-fry for 3 to 4 minutes until the rice is well combined. Stir in the kimchi and half of the prepared sauce (save the remaining sauce to serve) and cook for another 2 to 3 minutes, stirring frequently.

Once the rice is heated through and well coated with the sauce, push it to one side of the skillet, creating an empty space to cook the eggs. Pour the beaten eggs into the empty side of the skillet and cook for a few minutes, then slowly stir them for another minute. Once the eggs are almost cooked, mix them together with the rice mixture. Continue cooking and stirring until the eggs are fully cooked and evenly distributed throughout the fried rice.

Transfer the rice to a large serving bowl, drizzle over the remaining half of the sauce, then sprinkle with sliced scallions and black sesame seeds.

SUBS :
If you don't like too much spice, check the heat level of your kimchi before you add it to the rice. You can also reduce or omit the gochujang from the sauce for a milder version.

QUINOA BURRITO BOWL

These burrito bowls are colorful and vibrant, perfect for a relaxed and fuss-free brunch with friends. You can cut down the prep time by cooking the quinoa and beans in advance.

SERVES : 4
PREP TIME : 15 MINS
COOK TIME : 20 MINS

1 cup (170g) quinoa, uncooked, rinsed

1 tablespoon olive oil

1 (15-ounce / 425g) can black beans, drained and rinsed

1 (15-ounce / 425g) can pinto beans, drained and rinsed

1 tablespoon taco seasoning (taco spice mix)

2 ripe avocados

3 limes

½ bunch of cilantro, leaves picked

2 cups (180g) thinly sliced red cabbage

2 tomatoes, diced

6 radishes, thinly sliced

1¼ cups (110g) grated Monterey Jack cheese

½ cup (120ml) sour cream or Greek yogurt

2 jalapeños, fresh or from a jar, sliced

Salt and black pepper

Place the quinoa in a large saucepan with a lid. Add generous 1¾ cups (450ml) cold water and ½ teaspoon of salt and cook, uncovered, over high heat until it comes to a boil. Once boiling, cover with a lid, reduce the heat to low, and simmer for 10 to 15 minutes. You can tell it's ready when the quinoa has absorbed all the water and is soft and fluffy. Remove from the heat and gently stir with a fork to separate the grains. Set aside.

Meanwhile, heat the olive oil in a large skillet over medium heat. Add both cans of beans, the taco seasoning, and ½ teaspoon of salt and pepper, and cook for 5 to 7 minutes, stirring occasionally to heat the beans through and incorporate the seasoning.

Next, make the guacamole. Cut the avocados in half, remove the pits, and scrape out the flesh into a bowl, then add 1 teaspoon of salt and the juice of 2 limes. Finely chop 2 tablespoons of the cilantro leaves and add to the avocado. Mash the mixture well with a fork until you have no lumps.

TO ASSEMBLE :

Divide the cooked quinoa among 4 bowls (about ½ cup / 95g each), add ½ cup (45g) shredded red cabbage next to the quinoa, and a large spoonful of the beans. Keep all the ingredients separate from each other and create a layering effect with the toppings.

Next, add the diced tomatoes, remaining cilantro leaves, the sliced radishes, and cheese. Place a large spoonful of guacamole in the middle of each bowl, then a spoonful of sour cream or yogurt, and a few slices of jalapeño on top. Cut the remaining lime into 4 wedges and place a wedge in each bowl before serving.

SUBS :
Use any colorful vegetables you have on hand. Grated carrot, diced bell peppers, corn kernels, mixed greens, or pickled red onions make great alternatives or extras.

MAKE AHEAD BREAKFAST BURRITOS

Make these burritos up to a day in advance and just reheat when it's time to eat. These can be frozen for up to a month so they're ideal for meal prepping ahead of time and not just for parties.

SERVES : 6
PREP TIME : 20 MINS
COOK TIME : 30 MINS

1 pound (450g) streaky (lean) bacon slices

5 baby potatoes (about 12 ounces / 350g) cut into ½-inch (1cm) pieces

1 teaspoon smoked paprika

½ tablespoon olive oil

½ teaspoon sea salt

8 eggs, whisked

¾ cup (75g) grated Monterey Jack cheese

6 (12-inch / 30cm) tortillas

4½ ounces (125g) baby spinach leaves

3 tablespoons hot sauce or mild salsa

1 (15-ounce / 425g) can black beans, drained and rinsed

2 avocados, sliced

Preheat the oven to 400°F (200°C). Line 2 large baking sheets with baking parchment.

On 1 baking sheet, lay out the bacon evenly. In a small bowl, combine the potato pieces, paprika, olive oil, and sea salt. Toss to combine and spread out evenly on the other baking sheet. Bake the potatoes and bacon at the same time. The bacon will be ready in 12 to 15 minutes. Once crispy and browned, remove from the oven and cool. Stir the potatoes and check their softness; they will need another 5 to 10 minutes. Once cooked, let the potatoes cool.

Meanwhile, add the whisked eggs to a large nonstick skillet and cook for 4 to 6 minutes until the eggs are beginning to set. Stir and sprinkle with the grated cheese. Cook for another 5 to 6 minutes until set, stirring to keep fluffy.

TO ASSEMBLE :

Once all ingredients are cool, start to assemble your burritos. Lay out a tortilla on top of a 14-inch (35cm) piece of aluminum foil. Layer the ingredients in the center of the burrito, leaving a good space around the edges. You want the ingredients to form a 6 to 7-inch (16 to 18cm) square in the center of the tortilla. Use the spinach and bacon strips over the tortilla before adding the egg, potatoes, hot sauce, black beans, and avocado slices. Wrap your burrito by folding in the sides, then rolling up and over the ingredients to enclose and tightly wrap into a cylinder. Bring the whole burrito to the lower edge of the foil and roll tightly until enclosed. Pinch in the sides and push into the burrito to secure. Let the burritos chill in the refrigerator until ready to serve.

TO SERVE :

Preheat the oven to 375°F (190°C) and heat the burritos for 15 to 20 minutes, or in a toaster oven for 10 to 12 minutes.

FREEZING :

Freeze the foil-wrapped burritos for up to 3 months in a container or ziplock bag. Cook straight from frozen for 45 minutes, or until heated through.

SMOKED TROUT & PICKLED FENNEL SALAD

This salad is my go-to when I'm looking for something light, fresh, and easy to prepare, and it's perfect for brunch in the garden on a spring morning. If you can't find smoked trout, you can use smoked salmon or any other flaky smoked fish. Add extra greens and a variety of fresh herbs if you have them, and you can also add soft-boiled eggs to the top, yum!

SERVES : 4
PREP TIME : 15 MINS
COOK TIME : 5 MINS

1 whole fennel bulb, fronds
    reserved, thinly sliced
1 cup (250ml) white wine vinegar
2 tablespoons superfine sugar
3 continental or telegraph
    cucumbers
2 cups (70g) watercress
2 fillets (about ½ pound / 225g)
    smoked trout, coarsely flaked
1 bunch of radishes, thinly sliced
Scant 1 cup (200g) labneh or other
    soft cheese like ricotta or feta
¼ cup (40g) capers, drained
1 bunch of dill, coarsely chopped
1 tablespoon olive oil, or to taste
Salt and black pepper

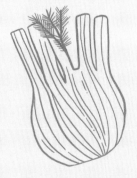

Start by making a quick pickle for the fennel. Place the sliced fennel in a bowl or jar, leaving the fronds aside to use later. In a small saucepan, heat the vinegar, 1 cup (250ml) water, sugar, and 2 tablespoons of salt over medium to high heat, stirring occasionally until the sugar and salt have dissolved. Remove from the heat and carefully pour the hot liquid over the sliced fennel, trying to submerge as much of the fennel as possible. Put the pickled fennel into the refrigerator to accelerate the cooling process.

To prepare the cucumbers, use a vegetable peeler to make long, thin cucumber ribbons, stopping when you get to the seeds. Flip the cucumber over and repeat on the other side. Continue with all the cucumbers, discarding the inside seed portion.

TO ASSEMBLE :

Assemble your salad straight onto a serving platter or in a large shallow bowl. Scatter the watercress evenly over the base of the platter, layer the cucumber ribbons on top, creating swirl-like shapes with them. Next, remove the pickled fennel from the refrigerator and drain off the pickling liquid (you can save the liquid for your next quick pickle). Scatter the fennel over the watercress and cucumber, separating the slices as you go. Scatter over the flaked smoked trout and sliced radishes. Gently spoon small chunks of labneh evenly over the salad, then finish with the capers, fresh dill, and reserved fennel fronds. Season with salt and pepper and a drizzle of olive oil to taste.

MAKE AHEAD :

You can make the quick pickle ahead of time. This recipe is best when you have a little more time for it to cool, but if you don't have much time, try the recipe on page 212.

PANCAKES
4 WAYS

A simple pancake batter can be adjusted easily. Try some of these alternatives to give your brunch table a little extra flavor and fun. If you don't want to be flipping pancakes at the stove while guests arrive, you can make these ahead, cover, and keep them warm in a low oven.

CLASSIC PANCAKES

MAKES : 16
PREP TIME : 10 MINS
COOK TIME : 15 MINS

2 cups (280g) all-purpose flour

2 teaspoons baking powder

2 eggs

2 cups (500ml) milk

3 heaping tablespoons butter, melted

Whisk all the ingredients together in a large bowl until the batter is smooth. Heat a large nonstick skillet over medium heat. Use a ¼-cup (60ml) measure to scoop a portion of the mixture into the pan. I can usually cook 3 pancakes at a time in a large pan. Cook for 1 to 2 minutes until lots of bubbles form on top, then flip onto the other side and cook for 1 minute. Remove from the pan, keep warm covered in a dish towel, and repeat with the remaining batter.

These are excellent served with the Whipped Maple Cinnamon Butter (page 115).

TIP :

If you have an air fryer, you can stack 6 to 8 pancakes at once. Line the bottom of the air fryer with a square of baking parchment. Heat the air fryer. Pour in ¼ cup (60ml) of the pancake batter and top with another square of baking parchment. Continue until you have 6 to 8 pancake layers, then cook at 350°F (180°C) for 3 minutes.

FROZEN BERRY SWIRL PANCAKES

MAKES : 8 LARGE PANCAKES
PREP TIME : 10 MINS
COOK TIME : 30 MINS

1 cup (150g) frozen berries

2 tablespoons superfine sugar

1 quantity of Classic Pancake batter

Combine the berries, 1 tablespoon of water, and the sugar in a small saucepan and heat gently to cook the berries, stirring and mashing slightly as they soften and the sugar dissolves. Simmer for 6 to 8 minutes, stirring occasionally to mash the berries down. Pass the berries through a strainer (in a rush I have left it with the chunks of berry, and it's just as delicious), then fold half of the berry puree into the pancake batter. Don't stir through too much, just drizzle over and quickly fold in.

Heat a medium skillet over medium heat. Pour ½ cup (120ml) of the pancake batter into the center of the pan. Once bubbles begin to form on the top, flip the pancake over and cook on the other side for 3 to 4 minutes. The berry puree will take a little longer to cook through on the second side. Use a spatula to press the pancake down and check it is golden before removing it from the pan. Repeat with the remaining batter, then serve the pancakes with the remaining berry puree to top.

LEMON RICOTTA PANCAKES

MAKES: 16
PREP TIME : 10 MINS
COOK TIME : 15 MINS

2 cups (280g) all-purpose flour
2 teaspoons baking powder
Finely grated zest of 1 lemon
2 eggs
1½ cups (370ml) milk
¾ cup (180ml) ricotta cheese
Butter, for greasing

Whisk the flour, baking powder, and lemon zest in a large bowl to combine. Add the remaining wet ingredients to a small jug and lightly beat. Pour the egg mixture into the flour mix and whisk until smooth. Heat a large skillet over medium heat. Use ½ tablespoon of butter to grease the pan. Once melted, scoop a ¼-cup (60ml) portion of the batter into the pan. I can usually cook 3 pancakes at a time in a large pan. Cook for 1 to 2 minutes until lots of bubbles form on the top, then flip over and cook the other side for 1 to 2 minutes. Remove from the pan and repeat with the remaining batter, greasing with more butter in between as needed.

TIP :
For an extra lemony flavor, serve the pancakes with Citrus Curd (page 209) or simply lemon juice and a sprinkle of superfine sugar.

BACON PANCAKES

MAKES: 8 LARGE PANCAKES
PREP TIME : 10 MINS
COOK TIME : 30 MINS

8 slices streaky (lean) bacon
1 quantity of Classic Pancake batter
Maple syrup, for serving

Cook your bacon to your preference, using an air fryer, oven, broiler, or skillet. Once cooked and crispy, lay the bacon on a plate covered in paper towels to absorb excess oil.

Heat a medium skillet over medium heat. Pour ½ cup (120ml) of the pancake batter into the center of the pan. Lay a slice of cooked bacon on top and once bubbles begin to form, flip the pancake over and cook the other side until golden. Remove the pancake from the pan and repeat with the remaining batter and bacon. Serve with maple syrup.

CREPE LAYER CAKE

This cake is a showstopper and very simple to prepare. Cooking the crepes takes some time, but this cake is best made the day before so on the day of your party all you need to do is take it out of the refrigerator and dust with confectioners' sugar. Voila!

SERVES : 8
PREP TIME : 30 MINS
COOK TIME : 50 MINS
CHILL TIME : AT LEAST 2½ HOURS

CREPE BATTER :

6 eggs
1 stick (115g) butter, melted and slightly cooled
2 teaspoons vanilla extract
3 cups (420g) all-purpose flour
2 cups (500ml) milk

FILLING :

1½ cups (370ml) heavy cream
1 cup (225g) mascarpone
1 cup (130g) confectioners' sugar
¾ cup (180ml) Citrus Curd (page 209)

Add all the crepe ingredients to a blender with 1½ cups (370ml) water and blend on high for 30 to 40 seconds, scraping down the sides to make sure all the flour is incorporated. Chill the blender for 30 to 60 minutes to allow the air bubbles to settle before you cook.

Heat a 9-inch (23cm) nonstick skillet over medium heat. Gently mix the crepe batter to reincorporate and pour ¼ cup (60ml) of the batter into the center of the pan. Pick up the pan and swirl to evenly distribute the batter thinly around the bottom of the whole pan. Cook for 1 minute, or until bubbles form on top and the edge is crispy. Flip over and cook for another 30 seconds. Stack the crepes as you cook the remaining batter. You should have around 24 crepes in total. Let cool.

For the filling, beat the cream and mascarpone together in a stand mixer fitted with a whisk attachment to soft peaks. While whipping, slowly add the confectioners' sugar until stiff peaks form. Fold in ½ cup (120ml) of your curd.

TO ASSEMBLE :

Layer 1 crepe on the bottom of a serving plate, then spread 3 tablespoons of the mascarpone mixture thinly over the top of the crepe. Continue to repeat with 24 crepe layers. Finish with a crepe on top and lightly cover before refrigerating for at least 1 hour. When ready to serve, top with a spoonful of the mascarpone filling and drizzle over the remaining ¼ cup (60ml) of the curd.

TIPS :

Use a little butter to grease your pan if you don't have a nonstick skillet. Once it's at the right temperature you should only need to reapply butter every few crepes.

Dehydrated citrus pieces or candied peel will add a stylish touch to your cake for decoration.

SUBS :

If you don't have any curd use 1 tablespoon each of citrus zest and juice. The flavor will be more of a hint than a punch but it will still be just as tasty.

MAKE YOUR OWN WAFFLES

Allowing guests to help themselves around a large platter or spread of food has to be one of the most relaxed and social ways to entertain. There will be no awkward pauses when there is a central table full of food to dig into. Guests can chat and eat at their own pace. The waffle batter is best prepared ahead and left sitting to thicken in the refrigerator, so can be made up to a day in advance. Cook the waffles and keep them warm in the oven or toast them when ready to serve.

SERVES : 6
PREP TIME : 40 MINS
COOK TIME : 30 MINS

1½ sticks (170g) butter, melted
    and cooled (set aside
    1½ tablespoons for greasing)
3 large eggs, lightly whisked
2 cups (500ml) milk
2½ cups (340g) all-purpose flour
3 teaspoons baking powder
2 tablespoons superfine sugar
½ teaspoon salt

WHIPPED MAPLE CINNAMON BUTTER :

2 sticks (225g) butter, cubed
    and softened
¼ cup (60ml) maple syrup
1 teaspoon ground cinnamon
½ teaspoon sea salt

Combine all of the ingredients in a large bowl and whisk together. Let the batter rest in the refrigerator for 30 minutes, or overnight. Heat your waffle iron and grease with melted butter. Spoon heaping spoonfuls of the batter onto the iron and cook until both sides of the waffle are golden brown and the waffle slides away from the iron. If you don't have a waffle iron, you can also cook these on a griddle pan in small rounds. Repeat with the remaining batter.

For the cinnamon butter, place the softened butter into an electric mixer and beat until smooth. Scrape down the sides of the bowl and add the maple syrup, cinnamon, and salt and continue to beat until everything is incorporated. Store in the refrigerator in a covered container or roll into a log in baking parchment.

TO SERVE :
· 12 waffles (store-bought if you don't have time to make the recipe)
· 2 to 3 cups (450g) mixed berries, such as raspberries and blueberries
· 2 bananas
· 1 roll whipped Maple Cinnamon Butter
· Maple syrup
· Nutella
· Whipped cream
· Citrus Curd (page 209)

TIP :
If the butter is refrigerated in a roll, then slice it into rounds and place on a small saucer on the table to serve on top of your waffles or pancakes.

BAKE &
SHARE

SHEET PAN BAKED PANCAKES

There is nothing better than pancakes for brunch. Although this is a simple recipe, it can be time consuming if you have a large group and want to make a lot. This recipe allows you to pop these into the oven and get on with preparing something else. Light and fluffy and rectangular, these pancakes make for a fun change.

SERVES : 4
PREP TIME : 5 MINS
COOK TIME : 18 MINS

1 stick (115g) butter, melted, plus
   extra for greasing
2 cups (280g) all-purpose flour
2 teaspoons baking powder
3 eggs
2 cups (500ml) milk

FOR SERVING :
1½ cups (150g) fresh berries
½ cup (90g) mascarpone
Maple syrup

Preheat the oven to 350°F (180°C). Grease a quarter sheet pan or baking pan, 9 by 13 inch (23 by 33cm), with butter and line with baking parchment.

Whisk all the ingredients together in a large bowl until smooth and there are no lumps.

Pour the batter into the prepared pan and bake in the oven for 16 to 18 minutes until golden all over. Let cool for 2 to 3 minutes before cutting into 3 by 4-inch (7.5 by 10cm) rectangles. Serve with your choice of toppings.

TIPS :
This recipe can easily be doubled or tripled if you have more people. If your oven is large enough, then make a half sheet pan size.

Once the pancake is cut into squares it freezes well. Wrap each serve in plastic wrap and freeze. Defrost and warm slightly to serve.

TOPPINGS :
- You can have a good variety of fruits or sides to go with your pancakes.
- Add Maple Glazed Bacon (page 164) or the maple butter (page 112).

BAKED BACON FRENCH TOAST

A classic French toast is one of my favorite brunch meals to cook. This baked casserole recipe hits all the good notes but is easier for a larger crowd because you don't have to fry each toast slice. You can make it the night before so all you need to do is bake on the day.

SERVES : 6 TO 8
PREP TIME : 15 MINS
COOK TIME : 60 MINS

1 tablespoon butter

1 loaf (1 pound / 450g) brioche or
    challah bread, cut into thick slices

1 pound (450g) bacon slices, cut into
    bite-size pieces

6 eggs

¼ cup (50g) soft brown sugar

1 tablespoon maple syrup, plus
    extra for serving

1½ cups (375ml) milk

1 cup (250ml) heavy cream

Grease a 9 by 13-inch (23 by 33cm) dutch oven with the butter. Halve each brioche slice and layer into the prepared dish. Set aside.

Fry the bacon in a large skillet over medium heat for 8 to 10 minutes, stirring occasionally so that all sides of the bacon are cooked and golden.

Whisk the eggs, sugar, maple syrup, milk, and cream together in a large bowl. Pour the creamy mix over the bread and turn the bread pieces so both sides are soaked. Scatter the cooked bacon over the top. At this point you can cover and refrigerate, either overnight or until ready to cook.

When ready to cook, preheat the oven to 350°F (180°C) and bake for 45 to 50 minutes. Check after 30 minutes. If the top and edges are browning too quickly, cover with aluminum foil. Once done, remove from the oven and let stand for 5 to 10 minutes before serving with extra maple syrup.

SUBS :
For a sweet version, add mixed fresh berries or other fruit and ground cinnamon instead of the bacon.

FROZEN BERRY DUTCH BABY

A Dutch baby falls somewhere in between a pancake and a Yorkshire pudding. It's a great alternative to pancakes as it cooks in the oven and saves you time standing over the stove flipping them. I love this because I always have some berries in the freezer, so it's easy to whip up. Serving the Dutch baby straight from the skillet creates a beautiful rustic touch for your brunch table.

SERVES : 4
PREP TIME : 5 MINS
COOK TIME : 25 MINS

¾ cup (175ml) milk

3 eggs

¾ cup (105g) all-purpose flour

2 tablespoons superfine sugar

1 teaspoon vanilla extract

¼ teaspoon salt

2 tablespoons finely grated lemon zest

½ stick (60g) unsalted butter

1 cup (150g) frozen blueberries

2 tablespoons confectioners' sugar, for dusting

FOR SERVING :
Maple syrup
Whipped cream

Preheat the oven to 425°F (220°C).

Using electric beaters, beat the milk, eggs, flour, superfine sugar, vanilla, salt, and lemon zest together in a large bowl for 3 to 4 minutes until the mixture is well combined and frothy. (This step also works well in a blender. Simply add the ingredients and blend on high for 20 seconds.)

Place a 12-inch (30cm) cast-iron or ovenproof skillet on the stove over medium to high heat and add the butter and half of the frozen blueberries. Let the butter fully melt and the berries heat through and start to soften. Once the butter has melted, pour the batter into the skillet and quickly transfer to the middle shelf of the hot oven. Bake for 15 to 20 minutes until deep brown and puffed up. Don't be tempted to open the oven during the first 15 minutes as this can cause your Dutch baby to deflate.

Carefully remove the skillet from the oven, scatter over the remaining blueberries, and dust with confectioners' sugar. Take the skillet straight to the table and serve your Dutch baby with maple syrup and fresh cream.

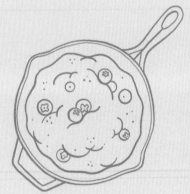

MAKE AHEAD :
You can make the batter ahead of time and leave it in the refrigerator, even overnight. Just make sure to bring it back to room temperature before you cook it as it won't rise if the mixture is cold.

SUBS :
You can use any frozen or fresh berries for this recipe; a mix would work fine.

BAKED OATMEAL WITH FIGS

This baked oatmeal slice can be made with any fresh fruit. Pears, oranges, or even frozen berries or mango if don't have fresh on hand. When eaten warm it has a chewy texture, which firms up and becomes crunchier if served at room temperature.

SERVES : 6
PREP TIME : 10 MINS
COOK TIME : 35 MINS

½ stick (60g) butter, melted, plus
    extra for greasing
5 to 6 fresh figs (about
    1 pound / 450g)
1 tablespoon superfine sugar
1¾ cups (175g) rolled oats
½ cup (40g) unsweetened shredded
    coconut
½ cup (80g) roasted hazelnuts,
    chopped
¼ cup (55g) light brown sugar
1 teaspoon ground cinnamon
1 teaspoon baking powder
2 tablespoons golden syrup
    or light treacle
2 eggs, lightly beaten
1¼ cups (300ml) milk

Preheat the oven to 350°F (180°C). Grease a square 8 or 9-inch (20 or 23cm) baking dish with butter.

    Slice 4 of the figs into ¼-inch (5mm) slices and use to line the bottom of the dish. Cut the remaining figs into wedges and set aside for serving. Sprinkle the superfine sugar over the figs and bake for 8 to 10 minutes to soften the fruit.

    Meanwhile, add the oats, coconut, half of the hazelnuts, the light brown sugar, the cinnamon, and baking powder to a large bowl and stir well to combine. Make a well in the center, add the remaining ingredients, and fold through. Pour the oatmeal mixture over the top of the baked figs and bake for 25 minutes, or until the top is golden and the middle has set. Let cool for 5 to 10 minutes before slicing, then top with the remaining nuts and figs to serve.

BAKE & SHARE

TIP :
Serve this with the whipped coconut cream on page 62 or a plain yogurt of your choice.

CARAMELIZED ONION & BRIE CROISSANT BAKE

The buttery croissants add another level of taste to this breakfast bake. It's also very easy to adapt for what you have on hand in the refrigerator. Make the onions for this dish up to 4 days in advance or use some alternatives listed below.

SERVES : 6
PREP TIME : 10 MINS
COOK TIME : 40 MINS

½ tablespoon olive oil
1 brown onion, halved and thinly sliced
½ tablespoon butter, plus extra for greasing
½ tablespoon balsamic vinegar
5 to 6 croissants
4½-ounce (125g) Brie wheel
5 eggs
1¼ cups (300ml) heavy cream
¾ cup (75g) grated Cheddar cheese
3 thyme sprigs, leaves picked
Salt and black pepper

Heat the oil in a small skillet over medium heat and sauté the onion for 6 to 7 minutes, stirring occasionally so that the onions are evenly cooked and don't catch on the bottom of the pan. Add the butter and vinegar, stirring to coat the onions, and cook for another 10 minutes or so as the onions caramelize. Use straight away or store in an airtight container in the refrigerator for later use.

Preheat the oven to 350°F (180°C). Grease a 7 by 12-inch (18 by 30cm) baking dish with butter.

Cut each croissant in half, then arrange the croissant halves side by side in the prepared baking dish. Cut the Brie into small slices and wedge pieces of the Brie into the dish in between the croissant pieces. Layer the caramelized onions over the croissants and cheese.

Whisk the eggs, cream, and salt and pepper to taste together in a small bowl. Pour the egg mixture over the croissant pieces, using a fork to press down some of the croissant bits if they are not submerged in the liquid. Top with Cheddar and thyme leaves and bake for 20 to 25 minutes until the egg mixture is set and the top is melted and golden brown.

SUBS :
- Make the fried bacon bits recipe (page 164) and substitute for the onions and Brie.
- Add halved cherry tomatoes.
- A simple ham and Cheddar cheese version of this tastes similar to a Croque Monsieur in a pan.
- Mix ¼ cup (50g) granulated sugar with 1 tablespoon ground cinnamon, then add this to the egg mixture instead of salt and pepper to make a cinnamon donut sweet bake.

BREAKFAST SAUSAGE CASSEROLE

All the best breakfast ingredients are mixed together and prepared ahead so you can just pop it into the oven the morning you are wanting to serve. There is nothing easier.

SERVES : 8
PREP TIME : 20 MINS
COOK TIME : 60 MINS

1 tablespoon butter, for greasing

1 (30-ounce / 850g) package frozen tater tots

1 red onion, diced

1 red bell pepper, diced

1 yellow bell pepper diced

1 pound (450g) breakfast sausage

1 teaspoon smoked paprika

8 eggs

1¼ cups (300ml) half and half (or low-fat cream)

1 tablespoon Dijon mustard

8 to 10 chives, finely chopped

2 cups (225g) grated mixed cheese, such as Monterey Jack, sharp Cheddar, and mozzarella

Flaky sea salt and black pepper

Preheat the oven to 400°F (200°C). Grease a 9 by 13-inch (23 by 33cm) dutch oven or baking dish with the butter.

Pour the tater tots into the prepared pan, sprinkle with flaky sea salt, and bake in the oven for 15 to 20 minutes until golden. Remove from the oven.

Meanwhile, heat a skillet over medium heat and add the onion, diced peppers, and breakfast sausage. Use a wooden spoon to break up the sausage as it browns. Add the paprika and stir through, then sauté together with the peppers and onion for 10 minutes, or until golden and cooked.

Whisk the eggs, cream, mustard, half of the chives, and salt and pepper to taste together in a small bowl.

Arrange the cooked sausage and vegetables in a layer over the cooked tater tots. Top with the cheese and pour over the egg mixture. Cover the dish with aluminum foil and let chill in the refrigerator overnight, or until ready to bake.

You can also bake straight away. Reduce the oven temperature to 375°F (190°C), cover with foil, and bake for 40 minutes. Remove the foil for the last 15 minutes of the cooking time. The egg should be set and the top golden. Remove from the oven and let stand for 10 minutes before topping with the remaining chives and serving with your favorite hot sauce.

SPINACH PIE

(V) (NF)

This pie looks incredible once it's out of the oven. The thin layers of flaky pastry created by the scrunched top of phyllo is eye-catching as well as melt-in-your-mouth.

SERVES : 6
PREP TIME : 20 MINS
COOK TIME : 45 MINS

1 tablespoon olive oil

1 red onion diced

1 garlic clove, finely diced

1 bunch of spinach, washed and
    leaves and tender part of
    stems chopped

1 bunch of dill, leaves
    coarsely chopped

1 bunch of mint, leaves
    coarsely chopped

6 eggs, lightly beaten

½ cup (120ml) sour cream

½ cup (125g) crumbled feta cheese

10 sheets phyllo pastry

1 stick (115g) butter, melted

Salt and black pepper

Preheat the oven to 350°F (180°C).

Heat the oil in a large skillet over medium heat and sauté the onion and garlic for 2 minutes. Add the spinach and cook for 8 to 10 minutes until softened. Set aside to cool, then drain any excess liquid from cooking the spinach and combine the spinach with the chopped herbs in a large bowl. Add the eggs, sour cream, and feta. Season to taste and mix together.

Use an 8-inch (20cm) round baking pan with a removable bottom or a pie dish. Brush each sheet of pastry with some of the melted butter and layer over the pan sheet by sheet. Lay the first sheet horizontally, the second sheet vertically, and continue with 5 to 6 sheets so that the bottom is well covered with no gaps. Pour the filling into the pastry-lined pan and fold the overhanging pastry over the top. Brush the remaining phyllo sheets with a little more butter, scrunch them, and place each one bunched together over the top to cover the pie filling completely. Brush with the remaining butter and bake for 30 to 35 minutes until the pastry is golden brown. Check the pie during baking and if it's browning too much cover the top with aluminum foil.

Let cool for 5 to 10 minutes before removing from the pan and serving. Slice at the table for added effect.

SHEET PAN CORN FRITTERS

Corn fritters are one of my regular brunch favorites. Converting this recipe to a one-pan dish means you don't have to spend the time frying and flipping individual fritters. Pop it all in a pan and then make some sides to serve alongside while it cooks. Sometimes, if I'm in a hurry, I add diced bacon to the mix, as it saves me cooking it separately as a side.

MAKES : 9
PREP TIME : 15 MINS
COOK TIME : 35 MINS

1 medium red onion, diced

1 medium zucchini, grated

2 cups (250g) fresh or frozen corn kernels

¼ cup (10g) cilantro leaves, chopped

1 cup (100g) grated cheddar cheese

1 cup (140g) all-purpose flour

1 teaspoon baking powder

½ cup (125ml) olive oil, plus extra for greasing

6 eggs, lightly beaten

1½ teaspoons sea salt, plus extra for the top

3½ ounces (100g) cherry tomatoes, halved

Black pepper

Preheat the oven to 325°F (160°C). Line a quarter sheet pan or a 9 by 13-inch (23 by 33cm) baking pan with baking parchment.

Add all the ingredients, except the tomatoes, to a large bowl and gently fold together until well combined. Pour the mixture into the prepared tray and spread out evenly. Scatter the tomatoes over and top with salt and pepper.

Bake for 30 minutes, or until set and golden on top. Remove from the oven and let cool for at least 10 minutes before cutting evenly into 9 pieces. Serve warm or cooled to room temperature.

SUBS :
You can easily use other vegetables and herbs in this fritter recipe. Swap the corn and cilantro for grated carrots or sweet potato and dill. Add diced bacon and asparagus pieces.

SERVE WITH :
- Herby Fig Salad (page 31) and Maple Glazed Bacon (page 164)
- Melon and Prosciutto (page 26) and Breakfast Chipolatas (page 166)

BAKE & SHARE

CHORIZO & ROASTED PEPPER GRATIN

This rich and creamy dish is very nice and warming on a cold day. Serve it with a leafy salad and your party is ready to go. The potatoes need to be very thinly sliced, so use a mandoline if you have one.

SERVES : 6
PREP TIME : 15 MINS
COOK TIME : 85 MINS

1 tablespoon butter, softened, for greasing
2 garlic cloves, minced
1 tablespoon chopped mixed oregano and thyme leaves
1½ cups (350ml) heavy cream
2 pounds (900g) russet or red royale potatoes, peeled and thinly sliced
7 ounces (200g) chorizo, sliced
1 (9-ounce / 250g) jar, roasted red peppers, drained
¾ cup (55g) grated Parmesan cheese
⅔ cup (55g) grated Cheddar cheese
Salt and black pepper

Preheat the oven to 375°F (190°C). Grease a dutch oven with the butter (I like this in a round dish or a skillet but it should be about 10 inches / 25cm in diameter and at least 2½ inches / 5cm deep). Combine the garlic, herbs, cream, ½ teaspoon salt, and ½ teaspoon black pepper in a jug.

Arrange a third of the potato slices in a layer in the dutch oven. Top with a layer of half of the chorizo slices and red peppers and a third of the mixed cheese and cream mixture. Repeat the layering, finishing with the potatoes and cream. Set the last third of cheese aside for after cooking.

Cover with aluminum foil and bake for 50 minutes. At this point use a knife or fork to check that the potatoes have softened. This will depend on how thin you've sliced them, so if your potatoes are still firm, cook for another 10 to 15 minutes. When the potatoes are cooked or close to, remove the foil, sprinkle the top with the reserved cheese and season to taste. Bake for 15 to 20 minutes until the top is melted, browned, and crisping.

MAKE AHEAD :

This is a great dish to prepare ahead. Set aside ½ cup (120ml) of the cream mixture with the last third of cheese. After the initial 50 minutes of baking, let cool to room temperature, then refrigerate covered until ready to reheat (1 to 2 days in advance works well). When ready to serve, remove from the refrigerator 1 hour before, pour over the reserved cream mix and the cheese, and bake for 20 to 30 minutes to make sure it's hot throughout.

SWEET POTATO FRITTATA MUFFINS

These muffins are a great choice for a picnic-style brunch. You can make these in advance and store in an airtight container in the refrigerator for up to 3 days. These make great lunchbox additions, too.

MAKES : 12
PREP TIME : 10 MINS
COOK TIME : 25 MINS

Butter or olive oil, for greasing
4 cups (640g) sweet potato, peeled and cut into cubes under 1 inch (2.5cm)
1 cup (160g) potato, peeled and cut into cubes
8 eggs, lightly beaten
5½ ounces (150g) goat cheese, crumbled
3 cups (90g) baby spinach, coarsely chopped
1 red onion, diced
½ cup (60g) grated Parmesan cheese
Sea salt and black pepper

Preheat the oven to 400°F (200°C). Grease a 12-cup muffin pan with butter or oil and line with squares of baking parchment.

Steam the sweet potato and the potato cubes for 5 minutes, or until just soft. Let cool slightly.

Add the eggs, goat cheese, baby spinach, onion, Parmesan, and salt and pepper to taste to a large bowl and mix together to combine. Add the steamed potatoes and mix.

Spoon the batter into the prepared muffin pan and bake in the oven for 20 minutes, or until set. Let cool for 10 minutes before removing them from the muffin pan.

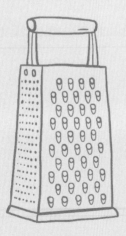

MAKE AHEAD :
You can make these muffins a day ahead of your party and store in the refrigerator. They are also good served cold.

HAM & CHEDDAR SAVORY SCONES

I love these savory scones, as they are wholesome, filling, and great to eat on the go or perfect for a brunch picnic.

SERVES : 4 TO 6
PREP TIME : 10 MINS
COOK TIME : 15 MINS

2 cups (280g) all-purpose flour, plus extra for dusting

1 tablespoon baking powder

1 tablespoon superfine sugar

½ teaspoon salt

½ teaspoon garlic powder

1 stick (115g) cold unsalted butter, cut into small cubes

1 cup (100g) grated sharp Cheddar cheese

4½ ounces (125g) ham, finely chopped

3 tablespoons finely chopped chives

¾ cup (175ml) buttermilk, plus extra for brushing

Line a baking sheet with baking parchment.

Add the flour, baking powder, sugar, salt, and garlic powder to a large bowl and stir to combine. Add the cold butter cubes and, working quickly, mix the butter through the flour mixture using a pinching motion with your fingertips. You want the mixture to be a crumbly, sandy consistency. Add the Cheddar, ham, and chives and stir with a fork to combine. Pour in the buttermilk, working it through the dry ingredients until it starts to come together to form a rough dough. Make sure not to overhandle the dough as this will result in tough scones.

Turn the mixture out onto a lightly floured counter and gently work the dough until it comes together and is easy to handle. If the dough is too wet, add a little flour, and if it's too dry, add a little extra buttermilk.

Transfer the ball of dough to your baking sheet and form it into a disk shape, about 8 inches (20cm) in diameter. Using a sharp knife or a bench scraper, cut the disk into 8 equal wedges.

Transfer the tray to the refrigerator to chill for 10 minutes before cooking. This will increase the height and flakiness of your scones.

Preheat the oven to 400°F (200°C). Using a pastry brush, lightly coat the top of the scones with buttermilk, then bake in the oven for 15 minutes, or until golden brown. Let cool on the baking sheet before serving warm with butter.

MAKE AHEAD :

These scones work well made in advance. Make and shape the dough and leave them, covered, in the refrigerator overnight. Just brush them with buttermilk and pop them straight into a preheated oven the next morning.

SUBS :

Cooked bacon or sausage can be great options to use instead of ham, or use fresh herbs for a vegetarian option.

CHEAT'S BENEDICT

The classic eggs Benedict is a brunch staple, but not so easy to make for a large group and in a hurry. This recipe will give you all the flavors and sophistication and take you no longer than 10 minutes to prepare and serve.

SERVES : 6
PREP TIME : 10 MINS
COOK TIME : 12 MINS

2 to 3 long ciabatta rolls
1 handful of baby spinach leaves,
   coarsely chopped
6 slices thinly shaved ham from
   the bone, halved
6 eggs
2 tablespoons finely chopped
   chives
Salt and black pepper

FOR THE HOLLANDAISE SAUCE :

1 stick (115g) butter
3 egg yolks
1 tablespoon lemon juice
½ teaspoon Dijon mustard
½ teaspoon sea salt

Preheat the oven to 350°F (180C). Line a large baking sheet with baking parchment.

Use a serrated knife to cut 2-inch (5cm) holes out of the bread rolls. Depending on the length of your roll you may fit 2 or 3 cutouts in each roll. You need 6 cutouts in total. You want to make sure you have a border of around 1 inch (2.5cm) around your cutout hole, and the hole should be at least 1 inch (2.5cm) deep. Make sure there is a thin layer of bread still underneath the cutout.

Arrange the rolls on the prepared baking sheet. Layer a small amount of spinach, then a slice of the ham in the bottom of each bread hole, making sure to press them down so that they are forming a cup shape around the bottom of the bread. Crack the eggs into a small cup, one at a time, and pour into the holes over the spinach and ham. Sprinkle each egg with salt and the chopped chives. Bake in the oven for 10 to 12 minutes. The eggs will continue to cook once they are out of the oven, so if you like a runny yolk, remove them from the oven earlier.

Meanwhile, make the hollandaise. Gently heat the butter over low heat in a small saucepan until just melted, making sure it doesn't boil. Whizz the egg yolks, lemon juice, mustard, and salt for 20 to 30 seconds in a blender. The eggs will blend and lighten in color. On the slowest setting, continue to blend the eggs as you slowly add the melted butter. Blend until all the butter is combined into a smooth and creamy consistency.

Once the rolls are done, remove from the oven, and let rest for 2 to 3 minutes. Cut the rolls into individual serves around each egg and serve on a large platter or individually with the hollandaise poured over the top and garnished with salt and pepper.

BAKE & SHARE

SUBS :
Try using brioche or even a croissant instead of the bread. Replace the spinach with another leafy green, and the ham with smoked salmon.

BAKED ONE-PAN EGG FLATBREAD

No bread, no worries. Make this quick flatbread dough and you can bake your favorite ingredients straight into it. You should have everything you need already in your refrigerator and pantry, and while it's baking you'll have time to set the table for your guests.

SERVES : 4
PREP TIME : 15 MINS
COOK TIME : 10 MINS

2 tablespoons olive oil

1⅓ cups (180g) all-purpose flour, plus extra for dusting

1 teaspoon baking powder

1 teaspoon sea salt

Scant 1 cup (200g) plain yogurt

5 to 6 button mushrooms sliced

2 handfuls of baby spinach, leaves coarsely chopped

4 eggs

¾ ounce (20g) Gouda cheese

Sea salt and black pepper

FOR THE GARNISH :

¼ cup (30g) Quick Pickled Onions (page 212)

3 tablespoons chopped flat-leaf parsley

Preheat the oven to 350°F (180°C). Grease a shallow baking pan or sheet with half of the olive oil.

Add the flour, baking powder, salt, and yogurt to a large bowl and mix with a spoon until combined, then use your hands to knead together into a smooth dough. Turn the dough out on a lightly floured counter and knead for 1 minute before rolling into a large rectangular piece, about 8 by 12 inches (20 by 30cm). Keep it a rustic shape but try to get to an even thickness of about ½ inch (1cm) throughout. Transfer the dough to the prepared baking pan, then use the bottom of a mug to lightly press 4 round indents into the dough. Arrange the sliced mushrooms around the edge of each circle. Fill each circle with the chopped spinach, pressing down slightly. Crack a whole egg into each of the circles and top with the remaining oil and season to taste with salt and pepper.

Bake in the oven for 10 minutes. The eggs will be set and the dough golden around the edges. Before serving, use a microplane to finely grate the cheese over the top, then garnish with pickled onions and chopped parsley.

BAKED PEARS WITH CRUMBLE

This recipe is a sweet favorite of mine and the pears can be swapped with any fruit in season. Simply adjust the cooking time depending on the fruit so that it can soften. Try peaches, quince, or apples, for a start. It's such a quick recipe and I always make extra as you are likely to go back for more.

SERVES : 6 TO 8
PREP TIME : 10 MINS
COOK TIME : 25 MINS

4 ripe pears (make sure they aren't too soft)
1 tablespoon unsalted butter
2 tablespoons maple syrup, plus extra for serving (optional)
1 vanilla bean, split in half lengthwise and seeds scraped out
Clotted cream or mascarpone, for serving

CRUMBLE TOPPING :
3 tablespoons unsalted butter, cold and cubed
¼ cup (35g) all-purpose flour
¼ cup (25g) rolled oats
¼ cup (20g) unsweetened shredded coconut
¼ cup (40g) soft light brown sugar
2 tablespoons chopped roasted hazelnuts

Preheat the oven to 350°F (180°C). Line a large sheet pan with baking parchment.

Peel and slice the pears in half, then cut or scoop out the cores. Melt the butter and maple syrup together in a medium saucepan. Add the vanilla seeds and stir through to combine.

Arrange the pears in a layer on the prepared baking sheet and spoon the maple syrup mix evenly over them. Bake in the oven for 10 to 15 minutes, depending on the ripeness and size of the pears. They are ready when soft enough to easily break with a spoon.

Meanwhile, for the topping, add the butter and flour to a medium bowl and use your fingers to rub the butter into the flour until the texture becomes even and sandy. Add the remaining ingredients and mix together.

Remove the pears from the oven and spoon the crumble mix onto each pear. Return to the oven for another 8 to 10 minutes until the butter melts and the crumble cooks and becomes golden. Serve with clotted cream or mascarpone and extra maple syrup as desired.

CINNAMON TWISTS

MAKES : 12 TO 14
PREP TIME : 5 MINS
COOK TIME : 15 MINS

1½ tablespoons ground cinnamon
3 tablespoons soft brown sugar
2 sheets ready-rolled puff pastry
1 egg, beaten

ICING (OPTIONAL) :

½ cup (65g) confectioners' sugar
½ tablespoon unsalted butter,
   melted
½ teaspoon vanilla extract
1 tablespoon milk

A good puff pastry is a staple in my freezer. It's soft and buttery with a warm crunch when fresh out of the oven and all done in 20 minutes.

Preheat the oven to 400°F (200°C) or according to the directions on the pastry package. Line a baking sheet with baking parchment.

Mix the cinnamon and brown sugar together in a bowl and spread evenly over one of the puff pastry sheets. Align the second sheet on top of the first, sandwiching the cinnamon mix together. Press down or lightly roll on top to secure to the bottom sheet. Use a paring knife to cut the puff pastry sandwich into thin rectangular strips. Work it out evenly depending on the size of your sheet. I like to make mine around 1 inch (2.5cm) wide by 6 inches (15cm) long. Pick up each strip and gently twist, slightly lengthening as you twist. Arrange the twists evenly on the prepared baking sheet. Brush each twist with beaten egg and bake in the oven for 15 minutes, or until golden.

Meanwhile, to make the icing (if using), add all the ingredients to a bowl and mix well until smooth. Pour the icing over the warm twists before serving.

JAM TWISTS

MAKES : 12 TO 14
PREP TIME : 5 MINS
COOK TIME : 15 MINS

⅓ cup (80ml) store-bought jam
2 sheets ready-rolled puff pastry
Confectioners' sugar, for dusting

Follow the above method using jam instead of the cinnamon mix. Once baked, let these cool slightly before dusting with confectioners' sugar to serve.

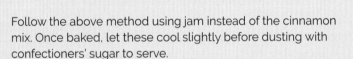

SUBS :

· You can use Nutella, peanut butter, compote (page 209), or hot chocolate powder inside these twists.
· Try some savory options, such as mustard, ham, cheese, or pesto.

BANANA LOAF CAKE

This is an easy loaf cake to prepare, and with a few extra touches for serving can be quickly restaurant quality. This recipe freezes very well so make 2 loaves at once and you will always have banana bread slices on hand.

SERVES : 8
PREP TIME : 10 MINS
COOK TIME : 50 MINS

1½ cups (225g) all-purpose flour
1½ teaspoons baking powder
½ teaspoon baking soda
½ teaspoon ground nutmeg
½ teaspoon sea salt
¾ cup (150g) granulated sugar
1 stick (115g) unsalted butter, melted
2 medium eggs
¼ cup (60ml) milk
1 teaspoon vanilla extract
3 medium overripe bananas
   (9 ounces / 250g), mashed
1 ripe banana, for topping (optional)

FOR SERVING :
Whipped coconut cream (page 62)
Honey, for drizzling

Preheat the oven to 325°F (160°C). Grease and line a 2-pound (900g) loaf pan with baking parchment.

Sift the flour, baking powder, baking soda, nutmeg, salt, and sugar into a large bowl. In a separate bowl, combine the butter, eggs, milk, vanilla, and mashed bananas. Fold the mixed wet ingredients into the dry ingredients, mixing until just combined. Pour the batter into the prepared loaf pan, slice the banana for topping lengthwise, and arrange on top of the batter. Bake for 45 to 50 minutes until a skewer inserted into the middle of the cake comes out clean.

Let cool in the pan for 5 to 10 minutes before turning out on a cooling rack to cool completely. Serve with coconut cream and honey drizzled on top.

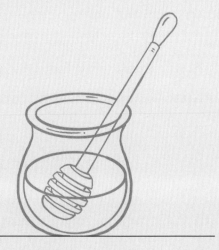

MAKE AHEAD :
You can make this loaf cake ahead of time, then when you are ready to serve just slice and toast individual slices.

QUICK MELT & MIX MUFFINS

These apple muffins can be adapted very easily to use any fruit or flavor. You can whip these muffins up so quickly and with minimal mess to clean up. Have them baking while you brew the coffee and voila, you're ready for guests.

MAKES : 12
PREP TIME : 12 MINS
COOK TIME : 15 MINS

1½ to 2 cups diced apple
(about 3 medium)

DRY INGREDIENTS :
2 cups (300g) all-purpose flour
2 teaspoons baking powder
½ teaspoon baking soda
½ cup (30g) unsweetened shredded
coconut (optional)
2 teaspoons ground cinnamon
(optional, depending on fruit
or flavor combo you are using)
½ cup (85g) soft brown sugar
¼ cup (50g) superfine sugar

WET INGREDIENTS :
1 stick (115g) butter, melted
1 egg
¼ cup (60ml) plain yogurt
½ cup (120ml) milk
1 teaspoon vanilla extract
1 tablespoon (15ml) olive oil

**CRUMBLE TOPPING
(OPTIONAL) :**
½ cup (70g) all-purpose flour
½ cup (85g) soft brown sugar
½ stick (60g) unsalted butter,
melted

Preheat the oven to 350°F (180°C). Grease a 12-cup muffin pan.

Add all the dry ingredients to a large bowl and stir well to combine. Whisk all the wet ingredients in a separate bowl. Pour the wet ingredients into the dry ingredients and fold in gently 5 to 6 times to combine. Overstirring can cause dry muffins so just fold enough to make sure the flour is mixed. Add the fruit you are using and fold a couple more times to evenly distribute. Spoon the batter into the prepared muffin pan. If using the crumble topping, mix all the ingredients together in a large bowl until it resembles breadcrumbs, then sprinkle 1 to 2 teaspoons of the crumble on the top of each muffin.

Bake the muffins for 15 minutes, or until golden on top and cooked through. To test if they are done, insert a skewer into the middle and if it comes out clean then the muffins are cooked.

TIP :
Cut 5 to 6 inch (13 to 15cm) squares of baking parchment and press them into the greased muffin pan to cook the muffins in. They will look like you've bought them in from your favorite bakery, but they'll be made by you.

SUBS :
You can use any fruit, nuts, or choc chips. Some of my favorite additions are banana and walnut, frozen berries, or poached quince or rhubarb (page 19).

CHOCOLATE OAT COOKIES

Who doesn't love to see a plate of cookies at a party? These oaty cookies are a twist on the favorite chocolate chip cookie. The oat and dried cranberry combination is perfect with a tea or coffee to end a brunch party. This dough is best made ahead so it's had time to chill a little before baking.

MAKES : 25
PREP TIME : 30 MINS
COOK TIME : 10 MINS

¾ cup (150g) soft brown sugar

¼ cup (50g) superfine sugar

2 sticks (225g) unsalted butter, melted and cooled slightly

2 eggs

1 teaspoon vanilla extract

2 cups (280g) all-purpose flour

1 teaspoon baking soda

2 tablespoons unsweetened cocoa powder

½ teaspoon salt

1 cup (100g) rolled oats

1 cup (150g) dried cranberries

Add the sugars and butter to an electric mixer with the cooled, melted butter and mix on medium speed for 1 minute, or until the butter and sugar have formed a smooth mix. Add the eggs and vanilla and beat until the mixture thickens and lightens slightly.

Meanwhile, add the flour, baking soda, cocoa powder, and salt to a medium bowl and mix together. Add the dry ingredients to the mixer bowl and mix on low speed until just combined. Add the oats and cranberries and fold through the dough. Chill the dough in the refrigerator for 10 to 30 minutes, if you have time. The mixture will thicken as it chills.

Preheat the oven to 350°F (180°C). Line a large baking sheet with baking parchment.

Use a tablespoon to scoop out a heaping spoonful of the dough (about 1½ ounces / 40g) and roll into a ball. Arrange the dough balls on the prepared baking sheet. Make sure they are spaced out. Use your fingers to press each ball into a larger flat circle and bake for 8 to 10 minutes until golden brown and spread out. Let cool before removing from the baking sheet.

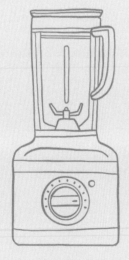

MAKE AHEAD :
This dough can be made a day in advance and stored in the refrigerator before you shape and bake. You can also shape the dough into balls and freeze for up to 2 months in an airtight container until you're ready to bake. Just remove them from the freezer and bring to room temperature before you pop them into the oven so that you can press down to a flatter shape.

SUBS :
You can make the cookies with or without the cocoa powder and swap out the cranberry and oats with nuts, chocolate chips, or different dried fruits.

QUICK
SIDES

VEGGIE BREAKFAST HASH

This hash recipe could be eaten at any time of the day, and I love it because you can use whatever veg you have in the refrigerator that needs using up. You can also add cubes of bacon, ground meat, halloumi, extra spices—really anything you have on hand to use. Dice all the vegetables in a similar small shape to make sure they cook quickly and evenly.

SERVES : 6
PREP TIME : 10 MINS
COOK TIME : 15 MINS

2 tablespoons olive oil

1 medium red onion, diced

5 medium red potatoes, diced

2 teaspoons paprika

2 teaspoons ground cumin

2 garlic cloves, crushed

2 tablespoons tomato paste

1 cup (120g) diced butternut squash

1 red bell pepper, diced

1 zucchini, diced

2 cups (160g) diced mixed
  vegetables, such as mushrooms,
  carrots, beans, kale, greens,
  tomatoes

1 (15-ounce / 425g) can cannellini
  beans or chickpeas, drained
  and rinsed

Sea salt and black pepper

Heat the oil in a large, heavy saucepan over medium heat and sauté the onion and potatoes for 6 to 7 minutes, stirring occasionally until the potatoes have started to brown and soften. Add the paprika, cumin, and garlic and stir through to mix well. Mix the tomato paste with ¼ cup (60ml) water and pour over the potato mix. Add the squash and remaining diced vegetables and beans. Set aside any leafy greens such as spinach or kale to add in the last few minutes of cooking. Season well and sauté for 5 minutes, stirring to coat all the vegetables in the spices. Add any last leafy veg and stir to toss through. Serve hot from the pan.

HASH BROWNS

There's nothing better to eat with eggs than a crispy hash brown. Making your own hash browns gives a more rustic feel and you get a mixture of soft and crunchy textures, which I love. Serve these with a bowl of soft-boiled eggs and slices of avocado and no one will be complaining!

MAKES : 12
PREP TIME : 15 MINS
COOK TIME : 26 MINS

1 medium sweet potato, grated
3 large russet potatoes, grated
½ cup (60g) grated Gruyère cheese
3 tablespoons all-purpose flour
Vegetable oil, for shallow-frying
Sea salt and black pepper

Combine the grated potatoes in a strainer. Squash out as much moisture as you can before adding to a large bowl with the remaining ingredients, except the oil. Season to taste.

Heat a large skillet over medium heat with a shallow layer of vegetable oil. Scoop about ⅓ cup (75g) of the potato mixture into your hands and squeeze again to make into a ball. Carefully place in the hot oil and flatten with a spatula to create a flat patty, about 3 inches (7.5cm) long and ½ inch (1cm) thick. Fry for 3 to 4 minutes on each side, pressing down with a spatula in between. Remove the patty from the oil and let drain on paper towels. Repeat with the remaining potato mixture. These are best eaten fresh but you can transfer them to a baking sheet, cover in aluminum foil, and keep warm in a low oven until ready to serve.

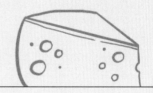

TIP :
If you have an air fryer, you can also spritz these with oil and air fry them at 425°F (220°C) for 6 to 8 minutes until crispy and golden. If you want to have these ready faster, use 2 large skillets and fry more at once.

SUBS :
You can make these hash browns using only russets instead of the sweet potato, too.

QUICK SIDES

SMOKY BAKED BEANS

These beans can be eaten on their own with crusty bread or as a side to a hot bacon and egg breakfast. Don't be put off by the long list of ingredients, they're all pantry staples and nothing you wouldn't usually have on hand. The longer these slowly simmer and sit together the better, so make them in advance and then reheat when you want to use. They will keep for up to a week in the refrigerator, too.

SERVES : 6
PREP TIME : 10 MINS
COOK TIME : 20 TO 60 MINS

1 tablespoon olive oil

1 brown onion, finely diced

3 garlic cloves, crushed

1 teaspoon mustard powder

2 teaspoons smoked paprika

½ teaspoon ground cumin

1 teaspoon ground chile or hot pepper flakes (optional)

3 (15-ounce / 425g) cans beans, such as black beans, red kidney beans, or cannellini beans, drained and rinsed (use 3 types of beans or all the same)

¼ cup (60ml) barbecue sauce

¼ cup (60ml) tomato ketchup

1 cup (250ml) tomato paste

2 tablespoons maple syrup

1 tablespoon apple cider vinegar

1 teaspoon salt

¼ teaspoon black pepper

Place a large saucepan or crockpot over medium to high heat. Add the olive oil and onion and sauté for 2 to 3 minutes, stirring occasionally until the onion is starting to turn translucent. Add the garlic and spices and sauté for another few minutes until the mixture is fragrant. Add the drained beans together with all the remaining ingredients and ¾ cup (180ml) water. Bring to a boil, then reduce the heat to low, cover with a lid, and simmer for 20 to 60 minutes. If you need the sauce to thicken, simply leave the lid off while the sauce simmers. The longer the beans simmer the more the flavors will develop.

TIP :
You can easily use a slow cooker for these beans, just reduce the water to ½ cup (120ml) and cook on low for 6 hours.

SUBS :
Add smoked bacon or ham hock for a hearty, meaty version.

MAPLE GLAZED BACON

SERVES : 6
PREP TIME : 5 MINS
COOK TIME : 20 MINS

1½ pounds (675g) streaky (lean) bacon slices
¼ cup (60ml) maple syrup

You can't think brunch without bacon making an appearance. The natural umami flavor of bacon combines salty, smoky, and juicy to create a mouthwatering savory treat.

Preheat the oven to 400°F (200°C). Line a large baking sheet with baking parchment.
   Lay the bacon on the lined baking sheet in a single layer. Set the timer for 10 minutes, then check how golden the bacon is. Depending on the thickness of the slices the bacon should be nearly ready and browning. When the bacon is 2 minutes away from the perfect crispness, brush the top with maple syrup. Bake for 2 minutes, turn over, brush the other side and cook for 2 minutes. Let the bacon cool on paper towels.

FRIED BACON WITH SPINACH

SERVES : 6
PREP TIME : 10 MINS
COOK TIME : 15 MINS

1 tablespoon olive oil
1 brown onion, finely diced
1 pound (450g) streaky (lean) bacon slices, coarsely diced (remember that it will shrink when cooked)
3 cups tightly packed (90g) baby spinach leaves

A quick alternative to the Maple Glazed Bacon above—fry the bacon in a skillet, then add the spinach just before serving.

Heat the olive oil in a large skillet over medium heat. Add the onion and sauté for 1 to 2 minutes. Add the bacon and fry for about 8 minutes, stirring occasionally to ensure it is cooking evenly. Once the bacon is looking golden and starting to crisp, add the spinach and stir as it heats and starts to wilt. Serve immediately.

TIP :
Both of these recipes can be prepared ahead and left with just the last finishing touches needed before serving. Have your maple bacon cooked, then brush the first coat of maple syrup while the bacon is out of the oven. Leave the oven on and just complete the last coat of maple syrup, then reheat for 1 to 2 minutes to serve. For the fried bacon, have the bacon and onion mix cooked and ready, then just reheat and add the spinach at serving time.

BAKED BREAKFAST CHIPOLATA

Chipolatas are a great accompaniment to a traditional hot breakfast. These flavorful sausages are smaller than a usual sausage and are traditionally made of pork. These are so quick and easy to cook, and baking them in the oven is mess-free and super simple.

SERVES : 6
PREP TIME : 5 MINS
COOK TIME : 17 MINS

½ pound (225g) streaky (lean)
   bacon slices
12 pork chipolatas
   (about 1 pound / 450g)
½ cup (120ml) smoky
   barbecue sauce

Preheat the oven to 350°F (180°C). Line a large baking sheet with baking parchment.

Cut the bacon slices in half and wrap half a slice around each of the chipolatas. You may need to use a toothpick to secure but often I find the bacon sticks on its own. Lay the wrapped sausages evenly on the prepared baking sheet and bake for 10 minutes.

Remove the baking sheet from the oven and brush each sausage with barbecue sauce. Return the baking sheet to the oven for another 5 to 7 minutes to finish cooking and it's all browned.

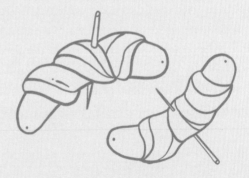

MAKE AHEAD :
You can cook these ahead of time and store them in the refrigerator overnight. Simply reheat in an oven preheated to 300°F (150°C) covered with aluminum foil, or in the microwave, when you are ready to serve them.

SUBS :
You can make these on their own without the bacon.

GARLIC & THYME MUSHROOMS

Mushrooms carry so much depth and flavor, perfect for a delicious brunch side. Warm and comforting, you can use this recipe as a toast topping to serve with eggs, or even to go along with a savory rice pudding.

SERVES : 6
PREP TIME : 5 MINS
COOK TIME : 15 MINS

2 tablespoons olive oil
1½ pounds (675g)
    button mushrooms
4 garlic cloves, minced
6 thyme sprigs, leaves picked
½ stick (60g) unsalted butter
Salt and black pepper
2 tablespoons coarsely
    chopped flat-leaf parsley,
    for garnish

Place a large skillet over medium to high heat and add the olive oil. Once the oil is hot, add the mushrooms (depending on the size of your pan you may have to cook them in 2 batches) and cook for 5 to 6 minutes; they will shrink and release moisture as they cook. Add the garlic, thyme, butter, and season with a generous amount of salt and pepper. Cook for another 6 to 8 minutes, stirring every few minutes to make sure the mushrooms cook evenly. Once they are all golden brown, remove them from the heat and transfer to a serving bowl. Sprinkle over the chopped parsley to garnish.

TIP :
I like to use small button mushrooms for this recipe as you can keep them whole and they will cook quickly. If you can't find them you can use cremini mushrooms, but you will have to halve or quarter them so that they cook through. A mixture of mushrooms is another great alternative.

SUBS :
• Most fresh herbs can be substituted for thyme and parsley. Rosemary, oregano, and sage all pair perfectly with mushrooms.
• Add different toppings such as hot pepper flakes, lemon zest, or crumbled feta for yummy variations.

QUICK SAUTEÉD KALE

A simple yet delicious side to whip up while your eggs are cooking. Sautéing kale quickly at a high heat tenderizes it perfectly. Don't worry if it looks like too much kale while it is raw—as it cooks it shrinks down significantly.

SERVES : 6
PREP TIME : 5 MINS
COOK TIME : 5 MINS

1 bunch of kale, washed
2 tablespoons olive oil
3 garlic cloves, crushed
4 scallions, thinly sliced
1 tablespoon hot pepper flakes
   (optional)
Salt and black pepper

Start by preparing the kale. Using a sharp knife, remove the thick inner stalk from each leaf, then coarsely chop the rest.

Heat the olive oil in a large sauté pan set over medium to high heat. Add the garlic and cook for 1 to 2 minutes until fragrant. Add the chopped kale leaves, scallions, and hot pepper flakes (if using) to the pan and sauté over high heat for 3 to 4 minutes, stirring occasionally. You will know that the kale is ready once the leaves are tender and a brighter green color. Season to taste with salt and pepper and serve straight away.

SUBS :
- Get creative with your additions to this kale—add lemon juice for a citrus twist, or just before serving top with Parmesan cheese or nuts, such as toasted slivered almonds.
- Use any variety of kale you like in this recipe, such as curly or Tuscan.

SOMETHING TO SIP

CITRUS ICED TEA

SERVES : 6
PREP TIME : 10 MINS
COOK TIME : 10 MINS
COOLING TIME : 1 HOUR
TO OVERNIGHT

2 lemons, peeled and juiced
1 cup (220g) superfine sugar
6 black tea bags
1 lemon, sliced into rounds
Ice cubes
1 handful of mint leaves

This iced tea is simple and refreshing with a strong citrus hit to it. Don't be afraid to adjust the sweetness depending on your own personal taste—simply reduce or add more syrup if needed.

Using a vegetable peeler, remove the peel from both lemons—try to avoid getting too much of the white pith. After the lemons have been peeled, carefully juice them and set aside ½ cup (120ml) of lemon juice for use later.

Add the lemon peel, sugar, and ½ cup (120ml) water to a small saucepan and bring to a boil, stirring to dissolve the sugar. Once the syrup has reached boiling point, reduce the heat to a low simmer and cook for 3 minutes. Remove from the heat, strain out the lemon peel, and transfer the syrup to a small jug or bowl. Let cool to room temperature.

In a large pitcher, steep the tea bags in 4 cups (1L) boiling water. Let stand for 5 to 7 minutes, then remove the tea bags. Stir in the cooled syrup and reserved lemon juice. If making ahead, keep this mix in the refrigerator until ready to serve.

For serving, add 2 cups (500ml) cold water, ice cubes, and the lemon slices to the pitcher. Pour into tall glasses filled with extra ice cubes, and top each glass with a few mint leaves.

MANGO POPPING GREEN TEA

SERVES: 6
PREP TIME: 15 MINS
CHILL TIME: 1 HOUR +

4 green tea bags
4 tablespoons superfine sugar
3 cups (750ml) mango nectar
Ice cubes
1 cup (220g) mango popping boba
    pearls
sliced mango, for garnish

Popping pearls are a fun addition to this iced tea, and you can buy them at Asian grocers or online. If you can't find them, then use fresh mango diced into small cubes.

Put the tea bags in a large heatproof pitcher. Boil the kettle, let the water cool for 4 to 5 minutes, then pour 4 cups (1L) over the green tea bags. Add the sugar and stir for 5 to 6 minutes as the tea steeps and the sugar dissolves. Remove the tea bags, then chill for at least 1 hour. Make this 1 to 2 days in advance and keep in the refrigerator.

When ready to serve, whizz the green tea mixture and mango nectar in a blender until smooth. To assemble your boba teas, add ice cubes to the bottom of 6 glasses, then pour about a ¼ cup (55g) of popping pearls on top. Pour the tea mixture over the top, garnish with sliced mango, and serve with straws and tall spoons.

MIMOSAS

Special occasion brunches call for a special drink to celebrate.
The bubbly fruity flavors of a mimosa are an excellent pairing for many
of the brunch recipes in this book, especially the richer egg dishes.

CLASSIC MIMOSA

SERVES : 6
PREP TIME : 5 MINS

1⅓ cups (330ml) freshly squeezed
   orange juice (about 5 oranges
   if making fresh)
1 (25-ounce / 750ml) bottle dry
   sparkling wine, prosecco,
   or champagne

Sometimes the simple classics are the best.

Half-fill your glasses with orange juice (about 1¾ ounces / 50ml)
and top with sparkling wine (about 3 ounces / 90ml). There is no
need to be too exact, I usually work on 1 part orange juice and
2 parts bubbles.

NECTARINE BELLINI

SERVES : 6
PREP TIME : 10 MINS

3 to 4 ripe nectarines
Juice of 1 lime
1 teaspoon superfine sugar
1 (25-ounce / 750ml) bottle dry
   sparkling wine, prosecco,
   or champagne

Similar to the classic, but with a sweet, fruity twist.

Make sure the nectarines are at room temperature as they will be
more juicy. Halve the nectarines and remove the pits. Place the
nectarine flesh in a blender with the sugar sprinkled over and let
stand for 5 to 6 minutes so that the sugar is absorbed and some
of the juices begin to leach out of the fruit. Pour the lime juice and
2 tablespoons of water over the mixture and blend until smooth.
Depending on the ripeness of the nectarine you may need to add
a dash more water to achieve a pourable consistency.

    Work on the same ratio of 2 parts bubbles and 1 part fruit mix.
Start with 1½ to 1¾ ounces (40 to 50ml) of the fruit puree,
then top your glasses with two 1½-ounce (40ml) shots of sparkling
wine. Pour slowly, as the fruit can cause the bubbles
to have extra fizz.

TIP :
A trick we're using throughout this book is to create a self-serve
area. Make a DIY mimosa bar with a few juice flavors, some fresh fruit,
and bubbles. If you have them, use some vintage or a special set
of glassware to add to the party feel.

LYCHEE & POMEGRANATE MIMOSA

SERVES : 6
PREP TIME : 5 MINS

Juice from 1 pomegranate (about ¼ cup (60ml) juice), seeds set aside for serving
8 canned lychees
⅓ cup (80ml) syrup from lychee can
1 (25-ounce / 750ml) bottle dry sparkling wine, prosecco, or champagne

This combination makes an instant party—it's sweet, tasty, and a major pop of color.

Blend the pomegranate juice, lychees, and lychee syrup in a blender until smooth. Work on the same ratio of 2 parts bubbles and 1 part fruit mix. Fill your glasses with the pomegranate mix and a small sprinkle of pomegranate seeds, then top with sparkling wine. Go slowly as the fruit may cause the bubbles to fizz.

GRAPEFRUIT SPARKLING ROSÉ PUNCH

SERVES : 6
PREP TIME : 10 MINS

1 (25-ounce / 750ml) bottle sparkling rosé
1½ cups (380ml) ruby red grapefruit juice
½ ruby red grapefruit, sliced
3 rosemary sprigs

Pretty and pink, use a crisp dry rosé to let the grapefruit flavors shine in this summery punch.

Combine the sparkling rosé, grapefruit juice, grapefruit slices, and rosemary sprigs together in a large pitcher and gently stir to mix well. Serve.

TROPICAL REFRESHER JUICE

A fresh juice is an excellent appetizer for the taste buds, and this refresher is sweet and citrusy—a cup of sunshine. Add a wedge of fresh fruit over the edge of every glass for a stylish touch. Paper straws can add a little extra "party" too.

SERVES : 4
MAKES : 1 PITCHER (1L)
PREP TIME : 10 MINS

1 pound (450g) pineapple,
   skin removed and flesh cut into
   chunks, plus extra for garnish
4 oranges, peeled
1 lime, peeled
2 to 3 mangoes (10 ounces / 280g
   flesh), peeled and seeded
2 to 3 passion fruit, halved
   and pulp removed
ice cubes, for serving

Press the pineapple, oranges, lime, and mangoes through a juicer. Add the passion fruit pulp to the juice and stir to mix through. Use an old milk jar or glass bottle to keep chilled in the refrigerator until ready to serve. Add ice cubes to your glasses when ready to serve.

If you don't have a juicer, you can blend all the ingredients in a high-speed blender. If blending, add 2 to 3 cups (500 to 750ml) filtered water and the ingredients to the blender. Once blended, push the liquid through a strainer or strain through a nut milk bag to remove all fibrous pulp.

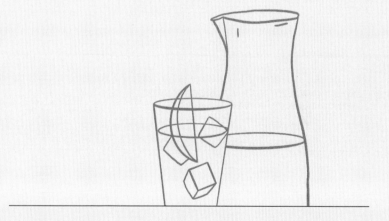

TIPS :
Juice can be made 24 hours ahead and kept fresh in the refrigerator. Cold-press juicers are more readily available now and juice that is cold pressed will stay fresh for longer. Give a good stir and garnish when ready to serve. Depending on the quality of your juicer, you may wish to pass through a strainer to remove pulp.

SOMETHING TO SIP

GREEN GOODNESS JUICE

Green juices feel like a healthy boost to the day but adding fruit makes them sweet and refreshing too. It's an excellent brunch pick-me-up and you can easily spruce up your serving pitcher with a few extra ingredients as a garnish.

SERVES : 4
MAKES : 1 PITCHER (1L)
PREP TIME : 10 MINS

4 celery stalks
   (about 10 ounces / 280g)
2 Lebanese cucumbers
   (10½ ounces / 300g)
3 curly kale stalks
4 green apples
1 lemon, peeled
3 mint sprigs
1-inch (2.5cm) piece of fresh ginger

FOR THE GARNISH :
Ice cubes
1 celery stalk
Lime slices
Extra mint leaves

Coarsely chop all of the fruit and vegetables, then press them through a juicer. Pour into a pitcher, stir, and serve chilled with garnishes as desired.

TIP :
Use a handful of fresh baby spinach instead of the celery stalks and replace the lime in the garnish with lemon, if you prefer.

OAT BERRY DELIGHT

The nuts in this help to make it a more nutritional and filling smoothie. Berries are a year-round constant in my freezer, but if you prefer to buy fresh and seasonally you can adapt this to add any fruit.

SERVES : 4
MAKES : ABOUT 4 CUPS (1L)
PREP TIME : 5 MINS

2 cups (300g) mixed fresh
   or frozen berries
3 cups (750ml) oat milk
2 handfuls of ice cubes
½ cup (50g) cashews
2 tablespoons honey
Strawberries, quartered, for garnish

Place the mixed berries, oat milk, ice cubes, cashews, and honey in a blender and blend until smooth. Divide among glasses and garnish with a strawberry quarter. Serve.

SUBS :
Use sliced banana, fresh or frozen mango, or pineapple chunks instead of the mixed berries, if berries are not in season. To make this vegan, replace the honey with maple syrup.

MATCHA PEAR SMOOTHIE

Matcha has a complex flavor and can be overpowering if used too liberally, but combining it here with black sesame, pear, and coconut makes for a subtle, sweet taste.

SERVES : 4
PREP TIME : 5 MINS

3 teaspoons matcha powder
¼ cup (60ml) maple syrup
2 to 3 pears, cored and coarsely
   chopped
2 large handfuls of ice cubes
1 cup (250ml) coconut yogurt
3 cups (750ml) coconut milk
1 tablespoon black sesame seeds
   or paste, plus extra seeds
   for garnish
Toasted coconut flakes, for garnish

Mix the matcha powder and maple syrup together in a small cup to form a smooth paste-like mixture with no lumps. Add the remaining ingredients to a blender, then pour the matcha mix over the top and blend until smooth. Pour into glasses or a large pitcher to serve and top with coconut flakes and more balck sesame seeds.

WATERMELON FRAPPÉ

SERVES : 4
MAKES : 1 PITCHER (1L)
PREP TIME : 10 MINS

1 pound (450g) ice cubes
2 pounds (900g) watermelon,
   seeded and flesh cubed
¾ cup (175ml) Greek yogurt
Small triangles of watermelon
   with skin left on, for garnishing

This icy drink is light and creamy at the same time. It's been one of my favorites since my school years. Cut your watermelon and store in the refrigerator, then blend just in time to set on the table. Watermelon can also be frozen in chunks so you can enjoy this all year round.

Add the ice cubes, watermelon, and yogurt to a high-speed blender and blend until evenly combined. Pour into a pitcher and serve. If you let the frappé cool in the refrigerator it will need to be stirred before serving as the drink will separate on resting. Serve, garnished with watermelon triangles.

TIP :
For a fun serving touch, slice down through the top of the watermelon triangles and wedge on to the glass rim.

MANGO FRAPPÉ

SERVES : 4
MAKES : 1 PITCHER (1L)
PREP TIME : 10 MINS

3 cups (360g) frozen mango
1 cup (150g) ice cubes
¼ cup (60ml) coconut yogurt
1¼ cups (310ml) coconut water

These ingredients are pantry staples for me. I like to make this super thick and creamy, almost like a soft-serve ice cream treat. It can be served as a smoothie or also as a smoothie bowl with some crunchy toppings.

Add all the ingredients to a high-speed blender and blend until smooth, adding more or less coconut water to achieve your desired consistency. Serve.

TIP :
I save any leftovers and freeze in ice-block molds for my kids to enjoy another time.

FRESH MINT TEA

SERVES : 1
PREP TIME : 2 MINS
BREW TIME : 5 MINS

1 fresh mint sprig

A good brew takes time. Allow at least 5 to 10 minutes for teas to brew.

Boil a pot of water. Add 1 mint sprig (about 8 leaves) for each 1 cup (250ml) water. Let steep for 5 minutes. Enjoy your tea.

SUBS :
Use other fresh herbs, which also make lovely fresh teas. Try thyme, sage, or oregano.

GINGER & LEMON TEA

SERVES : 4
PREP TIME : 8 MINS
BREW TIME : 5 MINS

2 lemons
1½-inch (4cm) piece of fresh ginger, sliced
2 teaspoons honey

Heating your teapot with plain boiling water for 5 minutes before your guests are due to arrive will keep it warmer for longer when the tea is brewed.

Juice one of the lemons and slice the other. Combine the lemon and ginger slices in a pot or heatproof jar. Pour over 4 cups (1L) boiling water and add the lemon juice and honey. Let steep for 5 minutes before serving.

MATCHA COCONUT TEA

SERVES : 2
PREP TIME : 2 MINS
BREW TIME : 5 MINS

2 teaspoons matcha powder, sifted,
   plus extra for dusting
¾ cup (180ml) coconut milk

Matcha whisks up smoother and foamier if you are making smaller batches, so make no more than 2 cups at once. Using coconut milk adds a little sweetness, which pairs beautifully with the matcha.

Use a small whisk to combine the matcha powder and 1½ cups (350ml) boiling water. If you have a handheld electric whisk, this saves time and produces an excellent creaminess. Warm the coconut milk in a small pan over low heat, then pour in as you continue to whisk. Dust with a little extra matcha to serve.

EARL GREY TEA WITH ORANGE

SERVES : 4
PREP TIME : 2 MINS
BREW TIME : 5 MINS

2 oranges
5 teaspoons loose leaf Earl grey tea
   (or 5 tea bags)
2 cinnamon sticks

FOR SERVING (OPTIONAL) :
Milk of choice
Granulated sugar

Don't pour boiling water straight onto the tea. Let cool for 2 to 3 minutes for black teas or up to 7 minutes for green and white teas.

Juice 1 orange and slice the other. Use a kettle to boil 4 cups (1L) water. Let the water cool for 2 to 3 minutes, then pour into a teapot with the tea, cinnamon, and orange slices. Add the orange juice, stir to combine, and let steep for 5 minutes. Use a tea strainer to pour into mugs or tea cups and serve with milk or sugar as desired.

BLACK COCONUT ICED COFFEE

SERVES : 6
MAKES : 1 PITCHER (1L)
PREP TIME : 5 MINS

1 cup (250ml) espresso black coffee
6 cups (1.5L) coconut water
Ice cubes, for serving

This is such a refreshing way to drink coffee on a hot day. You can prepare the recipe ahead, store in the refrigerator, and then quickly make a pitcher for guests to enjoy. Even if your guests aren't usually black coffee drinkers, they'll enjoy this naturally sweetened icy beverage.

Make 6 double shots of coffee (about 1¾ ounces / 50ml each) and set aside in the refrigerator to cool. Pour the cooled coffee into a large pitcher, add the coconut water, and stir to combine. Top off the pitcher with ice cubes and serve.

GRANITA LATTE

SERVES : 6
FREEZE TIME : 3 HOURS +
PREP TIME : 5 MINS

4 cups (1L) milk of choice
1 cup (250ml) espresso hot
  black coffee

Mix icy, flaky, cool milk with warm, freshly brewed coffee. Serve with a spoon so that your guests can eat in spoonfuls straight away or stir it all together to melt and sip.

Pour the milk into a shallow plastic container, cover, and freeze for 1½ to 2 hours. Remove from the freezer and use a fork to scrape the frozen milk into a granita. Return to the freezer until ready to serve. You can have this frozen for a few weeks in advance…the longer it's frozen will just mean a few extra minutes to defrost enough so you can scrape out again.
     When ready to serve, pour a double shot (1¾ ounces / 50ml) of hot coffee over each cup, then scoop out the granita evenly (a heaping ½ cup / 120ml each) on top.

TIP :
Save any leftover coffee from your morning coffee and freeze into large ice cubes. You can make a quick iced coffee by adding milk and topping with whipped cream. Watch the milk change color as the coffee cubes melt into it.

197

FROTHED MILK

SERVES : 4
PREP TIME : 2 MINS
COOK TIME : 5 MINS

2 cups (500ml) milk of choice

Frothed warm milk is essential in making café-style coffee. There are several methods to use at home to get a creamy frothed milk.

Calculate about ½ cup (120ml) milk for each cup. Warm the milk on a stovetop or in the microwave, being careful not to overheat. You do not want the milk to boil, as it will change the taste and scald the milk. The optimum temperature is between 140 to 150°F (62 to 68°C). This way it is also the perfect temperature to drink straight away. Use a handheld electric whisk, if you have one, to whisk the milk for 30 to 45 seconds. Tap out any air bubbles, then pour into your drinks.

Another tool you can use to froth milk is a cafetière or French press. Pour the warm milk into the plunger, then raise and lower the plunger under the surface of the milk, increasing the tempo as the milk volume increases. Plunge for about 30 seconds.

DIRTY TURMERIC LATTE

SERVES : 4
PREP TIME : 5 MINS
COOK TIME : 5 MINS

3 cups (750ml) almond milk
  (or other plant-based milk
  of choice)
1 teaspoon ground turmeric (or
  finely grate 1-inch / 2.5cm piece
  of fresh turmeric root), plus extra
  for serving (optional)
1 teaspoon ground ginger
1 teaspoon ground cinnamon, plus
  extra for serving (optional)
2 tablespoons maple syrup or honey
4 (1¾ to 2-ounce / 50 to 60ml)
  double shots of espresso
  black coffee

A dirty turmeric latte gets its name from the addition of a shot of espresso. You can also make this without the extra energy boost of caffeine too.

Heat the milk, spices, and sweetener in a medium saucepan over low heat, stirring constantly. As the milk warms, use a whisk to froth.

Pour the spiced turmeric milk over each shot of coffee, and serve with an extra sprinkle of turmeric or cinnamon.

BAILEY'S CREAM AFFOGATO

SERVES : 4
PREP TIME : 5 MINS
COOK TIME : 0 MINS

4 scoops vanilla ice cream
4 (1-ounce / 30ml) shots of Bailey's
4 (1¾ to 2-ounce / 50 to 60ml)
    double shots of espresso
4 pieces of biscotti or small
    cookies (page 210), for serving

This can easily be made into a hot coffee drink, like an Irish coffee. Just replace the ice cream with 1 cup (250ml) warm frothy milk.

Scoop the ice cream into 4 small glasses or bowls. If you can make up small plates or little trays with matching cups, line up 1 shot glass of Bailey's, a double shot of coffee, and the dish of ice cream. Guests can pour their own over the top of the ice cream once served. Adding a shortbread or biscotti is a nice touch but not necessary.

BOUNTY WHIP

SERVES : 4
PREP TIME : 10 MINS
COOK TIME : 0 MINS

1 cup (250ml) heavy cream
4 heaping teaspoons hot chocolate
    powder, plus extra for dusting
1 cup (250ml) espresso black coffee
2 cups (500ml) coconut milk,
    warmed and frothed

These can be made with either cold or warm milk. Top the cream with a dusting of chocolate to make a fun party-looking beverage.

Using an electric whisk, whip the cream until it forms stiff peaks. Prepare 4 cups with 1 teaspoon each of hot chocolate powder. Pour ½ cup (120ml) boiling water into each cup and stir to dissolve the chocolate. Add ¼ cup (60ml) black coffee to each cup, then top with warmed milk and a large scoop of whipped cream. Dust the tops with extra hot chocolate powder before serving.

SOMETHING TO SIP

QUICK ICED CHAI LATTE

This vegan chai latte is easy to make from scratch and will be ready and on the table in no time at all. I've served it in a pitcher for everyone to help themselves.

SERVES : 4
PREP TIME : 10 MINS
COOLING TIME : 1 HOUR +

4 black tea bags
1 tablespoon ground cinnamon
1 teaspoon ground nutmeg
½ teaspoon ground ginger
½ teaspoon ground allspice
½ teaspoon cardamom seeds
¼ teaspoon ground cloves
Pinch of ground black pepper
2 cups (500ml) cold unsweetened
   almond milk (or other plant-based
   milk)
1 teaspoon vanilla extract
¼ cup (60ml) maple syrup

FOR SERVING :
Ice cubes
2 to 4 whole star anise

Carefully pour 3 cups (750ml) boiling water straight from the kettle into a large heatproof pitcher or bowl with a pouring spout (not your serving pitcher). Add the tea bags, ground spices, and black pepper, then stir to combine. Let the tea bags and spices steep for at least 3 to 4 minutes.

In a smaller jug or bowl, make your milk mixture by combining the cold almond milk, vanilla, and maple syrup together. Stir and set aside.

Once the black tea bags have steeped for at least 5 minutes (the longer you leave this the more the tea and spices will infuse, creating a stronger flavor), remove the tea bags, squeezing the excess water from them with a spoon. Stir the mixture to help cool it down and refrigerate.

When you're ready to serve, pour the spiced tea mixture through a fine-mesh strainer into your serving pitcher (or divide it equally among individual glasses), add 2 large handfuls of ice cubes to the pitcher or glasses, pour over the almond milk mixture, and stir to combine the milk, tea, and ice. Top with star anise and serve immediately.

TIP :
For an extra caffeine hit add a few shots of coffee and make it a dirty chai.

PREP &
STORE

GRANOLA

Making homemade granola is so easy, I like to always have a full jar in the pantry. This is my base recipe but I change it each time slightly depending on ingredients I have on hand. Feel free to get creative and add extra ingredients and flavors, or swap out to different nuts or fruits.

MAKES : 4 CUPS (480G)
PREP TIME : 5 MINS
COOK TIME : 20 MINS

1½ cups (150g) rolled oats

½ cup (30g) shredded coconut

1 cup (120g) whole almonds, coarsely chopped

½ cup (50g) pecans, chopped

¼ cup (35g) sunflower seeds

¼ cup (35g) poppy seeds

1 tablespoon refined coconut oil

3 tablespoons butter, melted

3 tablespoons maple syrup

1 teaspoon flaky sea salt

½ cup (60g) dried cherries or cranberries

Preheat the oven to 320°F (160°C). Line a large baking sheet with baking parchment.

Combine all the ingredients, except the dried fruit, in a large bowl. Stir well to coat with the syrup, butter, and oil. Spread the mixture out on the prepared baking sheet.

Bake for 15 to 20 minutes until golden. After 8 to 10 minutes give the sheet a shake and stir to make sure it's toasting evenly. At this point sprinkle the dried fruit over so it toasts a little but doesn't burn. Remove from the oven once toasted and golden brown. Let cool fully before storing in a jar or airtight container.

TIP :
Make this vegan and dairy-free by omitting the butter and increasing the coconut oil to 4 tablespoons. Granola should last 2 to 3 weeks stored in an airtight container, but also freezes well. Just leave out to defrost to room temperature when you're ready to eat.

TAMARI SEED MIX

MAKES : ABOUT 1½ CUPS (210G)
PREP TIME : 2 MINS
COOK TIME : 6 MINS

½ cup (70g) pumpkin seeds
½ cup (70g) sunflower seeds
¼ cup (35g) black sesame seeds
2 tablespoons flaxseeds
1 teaspoons flaky sea salt
½ tablespoon refined coconut oil
2 tablespoons tamari

Use these sweet and savory toppings to add texture and flavor to simple dishes. Sprinkle them onto toasts, salads, yogurts, etc.

Add all the seeds and salt to a small bowl and stir to combine. Heat the oil in a large skillet over medium heat. If using a smaller pan you can roast the seeds in 2 batches. Add the seeds and use a wooden spoon to stir the seeds, so they don't burn. Once the seeds have begun to toast, add the tamari and give the pan a shake or stir to mix through. Let cool, then store in a jar or airtight container.

NOTE :
The seeds will begin to make a popping sound and become golden brown when toasting. They will burn easily so be quick and keep a close watch.

CACAO NUT CRUNCH

MAKES : ABOUT 2 CUPS (200G)
PREP TIME : 10 MINS
COOK TIME : 15 MINS

½ cup (80g) macadamia nuts
½ cup (75g) cashews
½ cup (30g) shredded coconut
½ cup (35g) quinoa or rice puffs
1 tablespoon refined coconut oil
2 tablespoons maple syrup
1 tablespoon cacao powder
   (or unsweetened cocoa powder)
1 teaspoon vanilla extract or ground
   cinnamon
Good sprinkle of salt

Add a spoonful of this chocolate crunch to Granola (page 205), use it as a topping for yogurts, or even sprinkle it over toast or bagels.

Preheat the oven to 350°F (180°C). Line a large baking sheet with baking parchment.
   Blitz the nuts and coconut in a food processor to chop the nuts into smaller pieces. Transfer to a large bowl and add the puffs
   Heat the oil, maple syrup, cacao, and vanilla in a small saucepan over low heat, stirring to combine. Pour over the nuts and puffs, stir well, and sprinkle with salt. Spread out over the prepared baking sheet and bake for 6 to 8 minutes until the edges are browning. Stir, then let cool before storing in an airtight container in the refrigerator for up to a month.

TIP :
Make your own chocolate bark with this nut crunch.
   Melt some dark chocolate and use a palette knife to spread into a thin layer over baking parchment, sprinkle generously with the nut crunch, and place in the refrigerator to set. Break into shards and enjoy.

MIXED BERRY COMPOTE

MAKES : 1 (16-OUNCE / 450G) JAR
PREP TIME : 5 MINS
COOK TIME : 30 MINS

2½ cups (300g) mixed berries, fresh or frozen
1 cup (240g) superfine sugar
1 apple, grated (keep skin on)
Finely grated zest and juice of 1 lemon

If you're a farmers' market shopper, you'll know that in season you can get large quantities of fruit really cheap. I love to pick a fruit each season and make some of my own compote with it. It adds a special touch to your brunch and your favorite fruit lasts through to the next season.

Combine all the ingredients in a saucepan, stir together, and let stand for 5 to 10 minutes. Bring to a boil, then reduce the heat to low and simmer for 25 minutes, stirring occasionally and using the back of the spoon to break up larger pieces of fruit.
Remove from the heat when the liquid has thickened slightly and started to become sticky. Cool for 10 minutes, then pour the compote into a sterilized jar. Cool and set before sealing with a lid.

TIPS :
To sterilize your jars, if you have a dishwasher, place the jars inside and run on the hottest temperature. Otherwise, clean in hot water, then place the wet lids and jars in a baking dish and let dry in an oven preheated to 350°F (180°C) for 15 minutes.
Store compote in the refrigerator for 3 to 4 weeks.

CITRUS CURD

MAKES : 1 (12-OUNCE / 360G) JAR
PREP TIME : 10 MINS
COOK TIME : 10 MINS

2 egg yolks
2 whole eggs
¾ cup (150g) superfine sugar
½ cup (120ml) citrus juice
1 tablespoon finely grated citrus zest
½ stick (60g) unsalted butter, cubed

One of my favorite curds to make uses ruby red grapefruit juice, as it still has the sourness of citrus but with a little added sweetness. You can make this recipe with any citrus juice and zest, though. Use this curd in muffins or with pancakes.

Place the egg yolks, whole eggs, sugar, juice, and zest in a heavy saucepan. Whisk together completely before heating over low heat. As the mixture heats, stir so that it doesn't cook too quickly and stick. Increase the heat slightly as the mixture thickens, about 6 to 8 minutes. Remove from the heat and add the butter cubes, stirring until the butter melts and the mixture is smooth. Pass the mixture through a strainer and into a sterilized 12-ounce (360g) jar (see above). Let cool to room temperature before securing with the lid and storing in the refrigerator for up to 3 weeks once opened.

CHOC CHIP FREEZER COOKIES

These cookies are delicious and the perfect sweet treat with a coffee or tea. It's a very simple recipe and there are endless flavor combinations to keep them different each time. The best thing about this dough is that it is baked straight from the freezer. Have a couple of rolls wrapped and frozen at any time, ready to have warm cookies on the table 10 minutes later.

MAKES : 12 COOKIES
PREP TIME : 5 MINS
COOK TIME : 12 MINS

½ stick (60g) unsalted butter, cold and diced

½ cup (65g) confectioners' sugar

1 cup (140g) all-purpose flour

1 teaspoon vanilla extract

1 egg

½ cup (75g) milk or dark chocolate chips

Add the butter, sugar, and flour to a food processor and pulse until the mixture resembles the texture of breadcrumbs. Add the vanilla and egg and pulse again until mixed through and the dough is beginning to clump together. Add the chocolate chips and blitz again so that the chips are cut into different sizes and evenly distributed through the mixture.

Tip the contents of the food processor onto a large piece of plastic wrap or baking parchment. Press any loose bits together and shape into a large roll, about 2 inches (5cm) in diameter. Wrap the cookie roll and freeze until you're ready to cook. If you make a few rolls, label them.

When ready to cook, preheat the oven to 350°F (180°C). Line a baking sheet with baking parchment. Remove the cookie dough from the freezer and unwrap. Cut into ½-inch (1cm) thick rounds. Lay the rounds spaced on the prepared baking sheet and bake for 10 to 12 minutes until lightly golden. Let cool for 5 to 10 minutes before serving.

SUBS :
- Swap the chocolate chips for ¾ cup (70g) crushed Oreos or any packaged cookies.
- Try adding ½ cup (40g) toasted slivered almonds and the finely grated zest of an orange.
- Try adding ½ cup (65g) pistachios and ¼ cup (30g) dried cranberries.
- Swap the egg in the recipe for ½ cup (115g) peanut butter and halve the amount of chocolate chips.

QUICK PICKLED ONIONS

Pickled onions are a very simple way to add a touch of fancy to your dish. The bright pink color they turn in pickling is an excellent styling touch and flavor boost for the dish. Perfect for jazzing up a salad, platter, or even toasts, they will keep in the refrigerator for weeks. I always like to have a jar of pickles ready to go.

MAKES : 1 (10-OUNCE / 280G) JAR
PREP TIME : 5 MINS
PICKLE TIME : 30 MINS+

1 medium red onion, halved and
thinly sliced
¼ cup (60ml) white wine vinegar
1 teaspoon superfine sugar
1 teaspoon flaky sea salt

Place the onions in an 10-ounce (280g) jar. Add the vinegar, ½ cup (120ml) water, sugar, and salt. Close the lid and shake to mix. Let the onions pickle in the refrigerator for about 30 minutess before you use. They will keep fresh for a few weeks but are best used in the first few days after you make them.

TIP :
Use a mandoline to slice the onions if you have one. The thinner the slices the better, but it does come down to personal preference.

SUBS :
Any vegetables can be swapped to replace the onion. Shaved fennel with dill is one of my favorite pickles, but you can also use sliced cucumbers, sliced carrots, or whole red chiles.

TOMATO CHILI RELISH

MAKES : 1 (16-OUNCE / 450G) JAR
PREP TIME : 10 MINS
COOK TIME : 50 MINS

1 large brown onion, diced
6 medium ripe tomatoes
5 long red chiles, diced (keep the seeds if you want extra heat)
2 garlic cloves, minced
1 green apple, grated
2 teaspoons yellow mustard seeds
1 teaspoon paprika
½ cup (120ml) cider vinegar
¼ cup (60g) soft brown sugar
2 teaspoons salt

This relish can be used on platters with cheese, spread on toasts, mixed into frittatas, or with eggs. It will elevate any dish with a flavor punch. Great to have on hand in the refrigerator at all times.

Bring all the ingredients to a boil in a medium saucepan. Reduce the heat, cover with a lid, and simmer for 40 to 45 minutes, stirring occasionally to ensure it's not too dry. The final texture will be quite jammy. The ingredients should have cooked down and most of the liquid cooked off. Turn off the heat and let the relish cool before transferring to a sterilized jar (page 209). It will last for up to a month in the refrigerator.

PESTO

GF

MAKES: 1 (10-OUNCE / 280G) JAR
PREP TIME: 10 MINS
COOK TIME : 0 MINS

2½ cups tightly packed (50g) basil leaves
1 good handful of baby spinach leaves
2 garlic cloves, minced
½ cup (70g) roasted cashews
Juice of 1 lemon
½ cup (40g) grated Parmesan cheese
1 teaspoon flaky sea salt
¾ cup (180ml) olive oil

At home I make so many variations of this recipe depending on which greens and nuts I have on hand. Lately I've been enjoying adding lemon juice and mint leaves for an extra fresh zing. You can use this spread similarly to the relish above—just fold through eggs, spread on toasts, or add to a dressing.

Add all the ingredients with just half of the olive oil to a food processor and blitz together until smooth, slowly adding the remaining oil until it's well combined and the spread is at your desired consistency. I tend to make a chunkier pesto base for brunches, so that it has some nutty texture, but you can also blend it for longer and add a little more oil to get a smoother consistency, if you prefer. Transfer to a sterilized jar (page 209) and store in the refrigerator for up to 3 weeks.

MENU PLANNER

SPRING

DRINKS
Iced Mango Popping Green Tea (page 174)

APPETIZER
Baked Rhubarb Yogurt Pots (page 19)

ENTREE
Baked One-Pan Egg Flatbread (page 142)

SIDES
Salty Citrus Salad (page 24)

DESSERT
Chocolate Cherry Bites (page 44)

SUMMER

DRINKS
Black Coconut Iced Coffee (page 196)

APPETIZER
Chocolate Chia Parfaits (page 36)

ENTREE
Waffles with berries & maple butter (page 114)

SIDES
Hash browns (page 160)

DESSERT
Sweet Twists (page 148)

FALL

DRINKS
Matcha Pear Smoothie (page 189)
Earl Grey Tea with Orange (page 195)

APPETIZER
Ricotta & Fig Croissants (page 54)

ENTREE
Soft Scramble with Labneh (page 88)

SIDES
Smoky baked Beans (page 162)
Serve with toasted sourdough

DESSERT
Baked Pears with Crumble (page 146)

WINTER

DRINKS
Dirty Turmeric Latte (page 198) plus extra black coffee

APPETIZER
Baked Rhubarb Yogurt Pots (page 19)

ENTREE
Caramelized Onion & Brie Croissant Bake (page 126)

SIDES
Bacon and Garlic Thyme Mushrooms (page 168)

DESSERT
Frozen Berry Dutch Baby (page 122)

VEGETARIAN

DRINKS
Fresh Mint Tea (page 194)

APPETIZER
Mango Yogurt Ripple (page 22)

ENTREE
Pesto Halloumi Stack (page 66)

SIDES
Quick Sautéed Kale (page 170)

DESSERT
Frozen Berry Dutch Baby (page 122)

VEGAN

DRINKS
Quick Iced Chai Latte (page 200)

APPETIZER
Granola Porridge with Poached Plums (page 82)

ENTREE
Quinoa Burrito Bowl using vegan cheese (page 102)

DESSERT
Peanut Butter, Strawberries & Sesame Toasts (page 48)

BRUNCH WITH THE KIDS

DRINKS
Oat Berry Delight (page 186)

APPETIZER
Ham & Cheese Savory Scones (page 138)

ENTREE
Frozen Berry Swirl Pancakes with fresh berries (page 110)

DESSERT
Banana Loaf Cake (page 150)

FAMILY BRUNCH PARTY

DRINKS
Watermelon Frappé (page 190)

APPETIZER
Sheet Pan Baked Pancakes (page 118)

ENTREE
Baked Bacon French Toast (page 120)

DESSERT
Chocolate Oat Cookies (page 154)

MAKE AHEAD–THE NIGHT BEFORE

DRINKS
Granita Latte (page 196)

APPETIZER
Choc Chip Freezer Cookies (page 210)
Quick Mix Muffins (page 152)

ENTREE
Breakfast Sausage Casserole (page 128)

DESSERT
Mango Coconut Rice Pudding (page 86)

MENU PLANNER

GIRL'S BRUNCH

DRINKS
Grapefruit Sparkling Rosé Punch (page 179)

APPETIZER
Overnight Oats (page 32) and Toasts (pages 64–5)
Smoked Salmon with Pickled Onions (page 52)
Sweet Blackberry Bagel (page 56)

DESSERT
Choc-dipped strawberries (page 44)

PICNIC IN THE PARK

DRINKS
Citrus Iced Tea (page 174)

APPETIZER
Fruit skewers (page 27)

ENTREE
Spinach Pie (page 130)

SIDES
Herby Fig Salad (page 30)

DESSERT
Salted Caramel Bliss Balls (page 40)

LAZY GRAZE BRUNCH

DRINKS
Black drip coffee and Mango Frappé (page 190)

ENTREE
Nordic Brunch Board (page 96)
Spinach Pie (page 130)

DESSERT
Sweet crunchy topping with vanilla yogurt (page 20)

FANCY DRINKS

DRINKS
Classic Mimosa (page 178)

APPETIZER
Fruit Plate with melon and prosciutto (page 26)

ENTREE
Warm Lentil Bowl with Egg (page 92)
Smoked Trout with Pickled Fennel Salad (page 106)

DESSERT
Bailey's Cream Affogato (page 199) or Crepe Layer Cake (page 112)

DAY AFTER BRUNCH PARTY DRINKS

DRINKS
Tropical Refresher Juice (page 181) and hot coffee

APPETIZER
Fruit Plate with papaya and coconut (page 28)

ENTREE
Sausage & Egg Breakfast Burger (page 72)

DESSERT
Chocolate Chia Parfaits (page 36)

INDEX

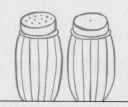

INDEX

ACKNOWLEDGMENTS

I'd like to send huge thanks to the amazing team that worked tirelessly to help bring this book to life. A big thanks to Hardie Grant and especially to Catie Ziller. It's an honor and such a pleasure to work with you. Thank you to the amazing design and editing team, Michelle and Kathy this book wouldn't exist without you. To the incredible food photography team, Lisa, Aya, and Giovanna, your hard work is so appreciated. Beautiful pictures to complement and complete this book. Importantly, to my family and close friends, for helping me cope with the stress of endless recipe testing and looming deadlines.

Hardie Grant North America
2912 Telegraph Ave
Berkeley, CA 94705
hardiegrant.com

Text © 2025 by Amelia Wasiliev
Photographs © 2025 by Lisa Linder
Illustrations © 2025 by Michelle Tilly

Published in the United States by Hardie Grant North America, an imprint of Hardie Grant Publishing Pty Ltd.

Library of Congress Cataloging-in-Publication Data is available upon request
ISBN: 9781958417768
eBook ISBN: 9781958417775

Acquisitions Editor: Catie Ziller
Photographer: Lisa Linder
Food and Prop Styling: Aya Nishimura and Giovanna Torrico
Designer: Michelle Tilly
Copy Editor: Kathy Steer

Printed in China

FIRST EDITION

MIX
Paper | Supporting responsible forestry
FSC® C020056

NORTH AMERICA